Donna Dewberry's
COMPLETE BOOK OF
One-Stroke Painting

2/10/98

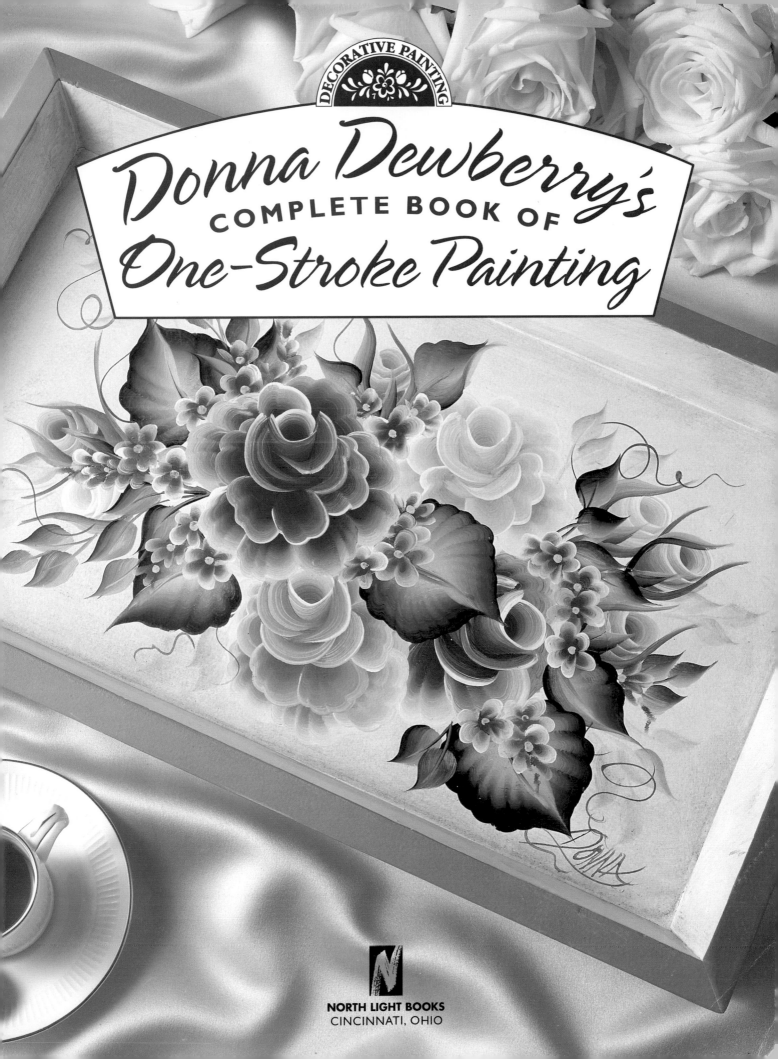

Donna Dewberry's
COMPLETE BOOK OF
One-Stroke Painting

NORTH LIGHT BOOKS
CINCINNATI, OHIO

A self-taught artist, Donna Dewberry's passion for painting began twenty-five years ago as a way to relieve the stress of being a wife and full-time mother of seven. Donna learned and perfected her One-Stroke technique at her kitchen table. Her stress-free and inspiring teaching style has taught hundreds of people all over the world the art of decorative painting, even when they never thought they could paint.

Donna has written eight books and numerous magazine articles teaching her One-Stroke technique. She continues to encourage people to paint, bringing out the artist in all of us.

Donna Dewberry's Complete Book of One-Stroke Painting. Copyright © 1998 by Donna Dewberry. Manufactured in China. All rights reserved. The patterns and drawings in this book are for the personal use of the decorative painter. By permission of the author and publisher, they may be either hand-traced or photocopied to make single copies, but under no circumstances may they be resold or republished.

No other part of this book may be reproduced in any form or by any electronic or mechanical means including information storage and retrieval systems without permission in writing from the publisher, except by a reviewer, who may quote brief passages in a review. Published by North Light Books, an imprint of F&W Publications, Inc., 1507 Dana Avenue, Cincinnati, Ohio 45207. (800) 289-0963. First edition.

Other fine North Light Books are available from your local bookstore, art supply store or direct from the publisher.
02 01 00 99 98   5 4 3 2 1

Library of Congress Cataloging-in-Publication Data

Dewberry, Donna S.
  Donna Dewberry's complete book of one-stroke painting / by Donna Dewberry.
      p.   cm.
  Includes bibliographical references and index.
  ISBN 0-89134-940-5
  ISBN 0-89134-802-6 (pbk.)
  1. Painting. 2. Decoration and ornament. I. Title.
TT385.D48   1998
745.7'23—dc21   98-11489
                                                                   CIP

Edited by Kathy Kipp and Heather Dakota
Production edited by Michelle Howry
Designed by Angela Lennert Wilcox

This book is dedicated to anyone who has a dream. If I were qualified to give advice, it would be as follows: "Don't give up on your dreams even when all odds seem to be against you and there just doesn't seem to be a way to overcome the obstacles." Pursue your ideas with all your body and soul, for it may be that one idea that opens the door to the realization of your dreams. Life is what we make of it. Every one of us has the ability to excel at whatever we wish. We are the only ones who hold ourselves back. Dream and work hard, because dreams really do come true. I know they do!!

ACKNOWLEDGMENTS

I would like to thank all those involved in the writing of this book, especially all of those patient, hardworking editors at North Light: Kathy Kipp, Heather Dakota, Greg Albert and Michelle Howry. I want them to know how much their patience and kindness have meant to me. They are truly a great group of people and my life has been enriched by their acquaintance.

I would like to further acknowledge the world of decorative painting, and the painters who have truly inspired me with their love and shared with me their talents. You have shown me a whole new world. We painters may be a small group in terms of numbers, but the impact we make on the world with our painting is as strong as any force. We can make the world a little more beautiful with our talent. That is, as my kids would say, an "awesome" responsibility.

TABLE OF CONTENTS

Introduction 9

Supplies 10

Preparing Surfaces 12

Introduction to Techniques

One-Stroke Techniques 14

How to Hold Your Brush 16

How to Load Your Brush 18

How to Paint Flower Centers 24

Bonus Project: Sunflower Birdhouse 25

How to Paint Flower Petals 29

How to Paint a Rosebud 30

Adding the Calyx and Stem 32

How to Paint a Shell Stroke 33

How to Paint C-Stroke Petals 34

How to Paint Leaves 35

How to Paint Branches and Grapevines 42

How to Paint Vines, Grass and Curlicues 43

Pouncing and Sponging 44

How to Paint Bows and Ribbons 45

Watercolor Shading 47

Watercolor Shadowing 48

Antiquing 49

Projects

PROJECT ONE

Garden Birdhouse Mailbox 53

PROJECT TWO

Watering Can and Clay Pots 63

PROJECT THREE

Ivy Keepsake Box 71

PROJECT FOUR

Rosebud Memory Album 79

PROJECT FIVE

Magnolia Floorcloth and Door Crown 85

PROJECT SIX

Wild Rose Birdhouse 93

PROJECT SEVEN

Fruit Cabinet and Plates 103

PROJECT EIGHT

Bouquet of Roses Serving Tray 117

Resources 126

Index 127

My Outlook on Decorative Painting

I really don't know where to start my story, so I guess I'll just tell you a little about my life. My husband and I have seven children; we consider them our best contribution to the world, and we love them dearly. They are each unique in their thoughts and actions, and each brings something special to our family as a whole. I often feel they are the inspiration for my painting.

The field of decorative painting is very similar to my family. Each painter has his or her own unique vision, and the techniques for accomplishing this vision—something created with talent and hard work. No two painters are exactly alike, nor should they be. Each of us has our own perspective on decorative painting. There are many different views of the same idea, and each one has its own place in the world.

I love to paint, and I want to share my interpretation of painting with others. I hope this book will help you in some small way, or perhaps even open up a whole new world to you. Painting has allowed me to pursue my dreams, and I know you can realize yours, too.

Good luck!

Always painting,

Donna

Supplies

Paints

I use FolkArt acrylic paints. They are rich, creamy and easily blended. These acrylic paints are high quality, artist grade, lightfast, permanent and waterbased (this makes them easy to clean up). For these reasons, I recommend them for the One-Stroke technique.

Brushes

The brushes used in all of my projects are the FolkArt One-Stroke brushes. The three-piece set includes a ¾-inch (1.9cm) flat brush, no. 12 flat and the no. 2 script liner. All of these brushes are synthetic (gold nylon). They were designed especially for the One-Stroke technique. The other brush I use often is the One-Stroke scruffy brush. Unlike other scruffy brushes, the design of this brush is even and uniform. This natural bristle brush has a great oval shape. You will find all kinds of uses for this brush. That's it! Just four brushes for all of these projects.

~ How to Clean and Care for Your Brushes ~

Cleaning and caring for your brushes will not only make them last longer, but will make them perform as they should. Every painter has their own method of brush care. This is how I clean my brushes. Please feel free to improve upon my method.

1. Thoroughly clean the brush with water using the grid in the bottom of the water basin.

2. Squeeze a cleaning solution into the bristles (I use Brush Plus by Plaid) and work it in with your fingers, making certain it is distributed all the way to the ferrule. When the Brush Plus is worked into the bristles thoroughly, rinse the brush with water. Repeat if needed.

3. Use a clean rag or paper towel to dry the bristles. Shape the brush as you dry it. Leaving a small amount of moisture in the brush won't harm it.

4. Lastly, I like to brush the bristles on a non-perfumed or non-deodorant bar of soap. This will keep the bristles in their correct shape. Make sure you rinse your brush before using it next.

Tips:

- Do not allow paint to dry on the brush.

- As you paint, rinse the bristles occasionally with water.

- Use a good quality brush basin.

General Supplies

Foam plate—I use this as my palette. Foam plates do not dry out the paint and are convenient to hold when I am painting.

Brush basin—I use a brush basin because it does not tip over easily. It is a good tool for cleaning your brushes.

Brush cleaner—There are many brands, but my favorite is Brush Plus by Plaid.

Household sponge—An oval-shaped sponge works best. These can be found in the household cleaning section of your supermarket.

Vinegar—I use white distilled vinegar; any brand will work. I use it to clean the galvanized tinware in preparation for painting.

Sponge applicator (brush)—a 1½-inch or 2-inch (5cm) sponge brush works best. They are disposable and inexpensive. I use them for basecoating.

Tracing paper—the size will depend on the project. I like the 11" × 14" (27cm × 35cm) size as it allows me to form it around the project and fits most of my patterns easily.

Transfer paper—I use white or black paper, depending on the basecoat of my project. You can find this at most craft supply stores.

Stylus—This is a great tool. However, if you cannot find one, use a ballpoint pen that has run out of ink.

Sealer—I prefer a spray sealer for most of my projects. The three I use the most are:

1. FolkArt Hi-Shine Glaze—clear lacquer-like gloss finish.

2. FolkArt Extra Thick Glaze—soft, subtle, glossy sheen.

3. FolkArt Matte Acrylic Sealer—soft, velvety-smooth matte finish.

Preparing Surfaces

Cleaning Your Mailbox
Clean the mailbox with damp paper towels or a soft cloth dampened with water and vinegar. Allow it to dry completely.

Cleaning and Basecoating a Terra-Cotta Pot
Clean the terra-cotta pot with soap and water. Let it dry thoroughly. With a sponge applicator, apply the basecoat around the circumference of the pot. Keep in mind that the moisture of the paint is absorbed quickly by the terra-cotta, so you need to work fast.

Either basecoat the inside of the pot with paint or apply a clear sealer, such as a waterseal product.

Preparing Wood for Painting

1. Any nail holes should be filled with wood filler. The wood should be sanded well to prepare the surface for the basecoat.

2. Apply your basecoat color using a sponge brush. Allow this to dry. Then apply a second coat.

3. After you have basecoated the Ivy Keepsake Box, dampen a sponge and rub it into Harvest Gold. Apply this color around the edges. Be sure to rub a little darker on the edge and lighter toward the center. This will give a nice antiqued look to the box. Apply this technique on the base and the lid of the box.

4. You are now ready to transfer the pattern onto the box.

Preparing the Floorcloth

1. Lay the floorcloth on a flat surface. Be sure to protect your working surface with a tarp or newspapers. Apply two or three coats of Wicker White depending on how porous the cloth is. Allow the paint to dry.

2. Transfer the pattern to the floorcloth. Remember—you may need to repeat the pattern a number of times (depending on the size of the floorcloth).

3. Dampen a flat sponge and load it with Butter Pecan. Apply the paint with any number of techniques to achieve the desired antique look. You can dab, swirl or pounce the Butter Pecan, but be creative and apply a finish you like. Let your sponging dry completely. You need to apply the antiquing at least an inch beyond the actual border. It is not critical to keep the border exact, as the center will overlap it.

4. Apply masking tape or drafting tape (preferably the easy release type) to form the center. Make sure the tape is adhered on the inside of the center, so the paint will not bleed under it. Apply two or three coats of Green Forest. You can use a brush or a roller: I used the One-Stroke Pattern Placement Guide Roller to apply the paint. Allow this to dry and remove the tape slowly and carefully.

Introduction to Techniques

My painting technique developed from my own desire to learn how to paint. I had a lot of interest, but little time or money. I embarked on what seemed like an impossible task—teaching myself to paint.

I purchased some brushes and paint and began working at my kitchen table. At first, I was not a star student. I practiced stroke after stroke, but didn't seem to make any headway. In fact, a teacher surely would have given up on me. Then one evening I had a revelation—I discovered that I needed to be myself, and decided to paint things as I saw them. I had finally found my niche in the painting world.

I learned an important lesson that night. *I* was the only one holding me back. As time progressed, I learned that many other painters experience the same frustration I did. The One-Stroke techniques I have developed are a way to make painting accessible and understandable for everyone. Whether you're a beginner or a more advanced painter, I hope these techniques will open up the world of decorative painting for you.

How to Paint Flower Centers
◀ PAGE 24

Sunflower Birdhouse
PAGE 25 ▶

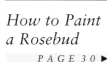

How to Paint Flower Petals
◀ PAGE 29

How to Hold Your Brush
PAGE 16 ▶

How to Paint a Rosebud
PAGE 30 ▶

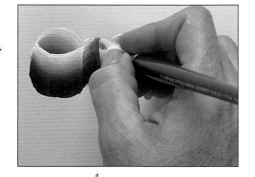

How to Load Your Brush
◀ PAGE 18

Adding the Calyx and Stem
◀ PAGE 32

*How to Paint
a Shell Stroke*
◄ P A G E 3 3

*Pouncing and
Sponging*
◄ P A G E 4 4

*How to Paint
C-Stroke
Petals*
P A G E 3 4 ►

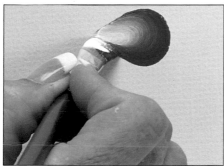

*How to Paint
Bows and
Ribbons*
P A G E 4 5 ►

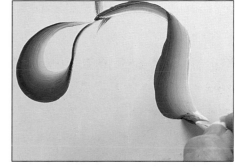

*How to Paint
Leaves*
◄ P A G E 3 5

*Watercolor
Shading*
◄ P A G E 4 7

*How to Paint
Branches and
Grapevines*
P A G E 4 2 ►

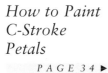

*Watercolor
Shadowing*
P A G E 4 8 ►

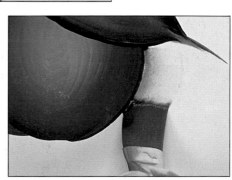

*How to Paint
Vines, Grass
and Curlicues*
◄ P A G E 4 3

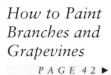

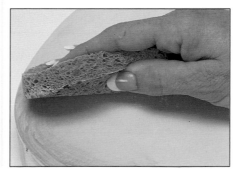

Antiquing
◄ P A G E 4 9

How to Hold Your Brush

Parts of the Brush

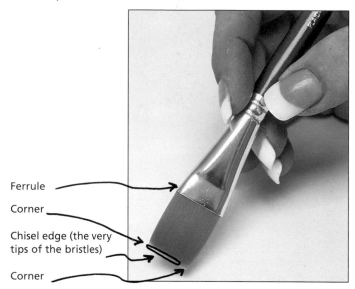

Ferrule

Corner

Chisel edge (the very
tips of the bristles)

Corner

How to Hold the Flat Brush

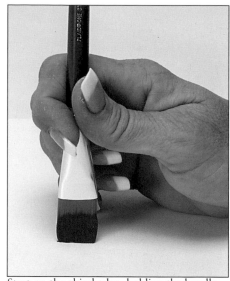

Start on the chisel edge, holding the handle
straight up.

Push

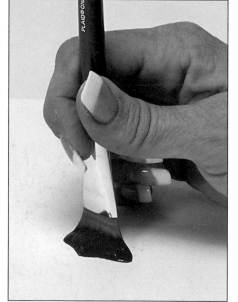

1 Push down on the bristles.

Turn

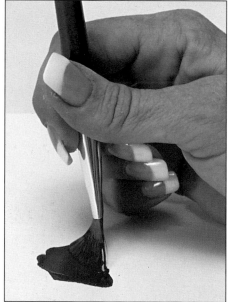

2 Wiggle the bristles to the right, pivoting on
one corner.

Lift

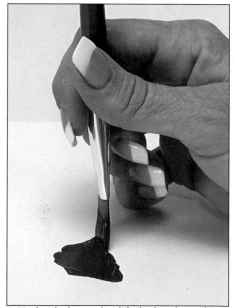

3 To finish the stroke, lift the brush until it
stands on its chisel edge. Only the very tips of
the bristles should be in contact with the
surface.

How to Hold the Script Liner

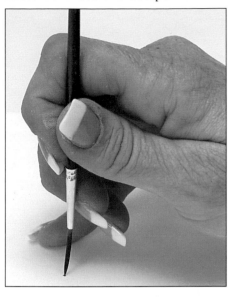

1 Holding the handle straight up, brace your little finger against the surface to keep the brush on its tip.

2 Use your little finger to help guide the brushstroke.

How to Hold the Scruffy Brush

Hold the brush handle straight up.

Pounce

1 When the brush is loaded with paint, pounce it straight up and down with a steady, firm motion.

Angle

2 To taper off your brushstroke, angle the brush so it rests on the long edge of the bristles.

Corner

3 To cover a very small area, use the corner edge of the scruffy brush to pounce lightly.

How to Load Your Brush

How Much Paint on the Palette?

Pour out enough paint to make at least a 1"
(2.5cm) puddle of each color you need.

Loading the Flat Brush

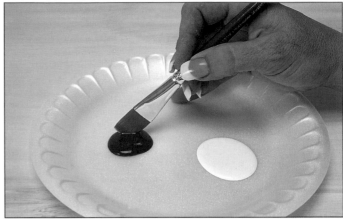

1 Dip one corner of your brush into the first color.

2 Turn the brush over and dip the other corner into the second color.

3 To fully load the brush, stroke it back and forth on the palette.

4 Repeat this two or three times to load the bristles with paint two-thirds of the way up to the ferrule.

5 Now that your brush is loaded, pick up paint on each corner to begin painting. Don't stroke the brush anymore on the palette. As you continue to work, load the paint only on the corners of the brush.

Multi-Loading the Flat Brush

1 Fully load the brush with two colors.

2 Pick up the lightest color (in this case, yellow) on the lighter side of the brush.

3 Pick up the darker color (brown here) on the darker side of the brush. As you paint, reload your brush by picking up both colors on each corner. Do not reblend the colors.

Double Loading the Scruffy Brush

1 Load half the brush by pouncing into the edge of the first puddle of color. Then pounce the other half of the scruffy brush into the edge of the second puddle of color.

2 The two colors should always be separate on the brush when reloading, as shown here.

Multi-Loading the Scruffy Brush

1 Pounce the lighter corner of the brush into the lightest color.

2 Pounce the darker corner of the brush into the darker color. As you paint, always reload by picking up both colors on each corner, just as you do with the flat brush.

Loading the Script Liner

Wrong! Do *not* load your script liner from the center of the paint puddle.

Right! Dip your script liner into water and pull paint from the *side* of the paint puddle, mixing the paint with your wet script liner.

Repeat this two or three times to make an "inky" consistency of paint.

Roll your brush as you pull it out of the puddle of inky paint. This will prevent it from dripping.

Using the Brush Handle to Make Dots

 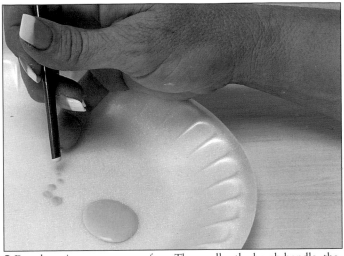

1 Dip the tip of the brush handle into the paint puddle.

2 Dot the paint onto your surface. The smaller the brush handle, the smaller the dots. You may need to reload to keep the size of the dots consistent.

Side Loading Your Brush

Wet your brush and stroke it along the *side* of the puddle of paint. The bristles are now loaded, one side with water and the other with paint. This gives a soft edge to your brushstroke. As you reload, always dip the same side of the brush into the paint.

How to Paint Flower Centers

Sunflower Center

Using a scruffy brush, double loaded with Maple Syrup and Licorice, pounce in an oval shape with the brown side of the brush always facing upward.

Adding Petals

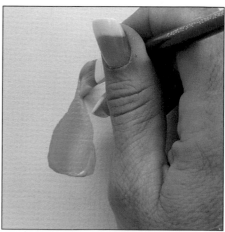

While the center is still wet, use a no. 12 flat brush double loaded with School Bus Yellow and Harvest Gold to stroke the sunflower petals from the wet center out. Grab the wet paint from the center and pull it out to form the petal.

Sunflower Petals

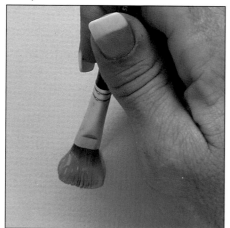

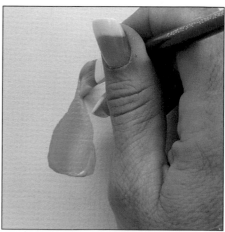

1 Double load a no. 12 flat brush with School Bus Yellow and Harvest Gold. Starting on the chisel edge, push down on the bristles.

2 Turn the Harvest Gold toward the point of the petal.

3 Lift the brush to its chisel edge to bring the petal to a point.

4 Repeat this grab-and-pull motion for each petal, working your way around the oval center.

5 If your center dries or loses its shape from stroking out the petals, re-pounce the center with wet paint.

Bonus Project: Sunflower Birdhouse

⟿ Color Palette ⟿

#938 Licorice

#945 Maple Syrup

#434 Berry Wine

#917 Harvest Gold

#736 School Bus Yellow

#448 Green Forest

#901 Wicker White

This pattern may be hand-traced or photo-copied for personal use only. Enlarge at 111% to return the image to full size.

Sunflower Birdhouse—side

Daisy Center

1 Pounce, using a corner of the scruffy brush loaded with Maple Syrup.

2 Pick up Harvest Gold on the same corner of the brush, and pounce a small amount to highlight the center.

Wild Rose Center

1 Pounce Green Forest with the scruffy brush.

2 Pick up a small amount of School Bus Yellow on the corner, and pounce to highlight the center.

Wildflower Center

Use the end of the brush handle dipped in School Bus Yellow to make a dot in the center of the wildflower.

How to Paint Flower Petals

Chisel-Edge Petals

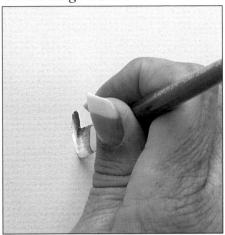 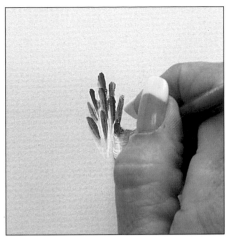

1 Double load a no. 12 flat brush with Wicker White and Dioxazine Purple. Standing the brush lightly on its chisel edge, make a short stroke down, leading with the white corner of the brush.

2 Walk the chisel edge in layers, from left to right and top to bottom.

Small Daisy Petals

Double load a no. 12 flat brush with Wicker White and Berry Wine. Starting on the chisel edge, push the bristles down lightly and stroke toward the center, leading with the white corner of the brush.

Large Daisy Petals

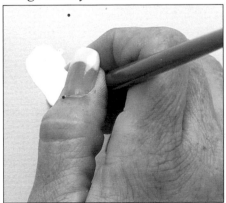 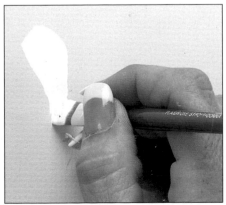 

1 Fully load a no. 12 flat brush with Wicker White. Starting on the chisel edge, push down on the bristles as you stroke the widest part of the petal.

2 Bring the brush back up to its chisel edge to pull the edge of the paint into the center.

3 Curve the strokes in different directions to form a more natural-looking blossom. All the petals should meet in the center.

How to Paint a Rosebud

Start With the Upper Petal

  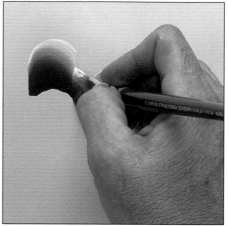

1 Double load a no. 12 flat brush with Wicker White and Berry Wine. Start on the chisel edge with the white corner facing upward.

2 Push down lightly on the bristles and stroke your brush up and over, with the white always facing upward.

3 Slide down on the chisel edge to finish the stroke.

Now Paint the Lower Petal

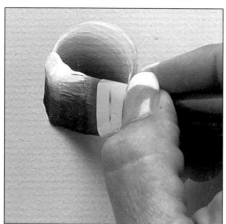 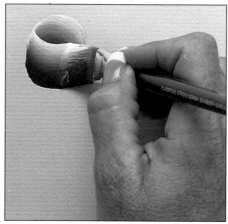 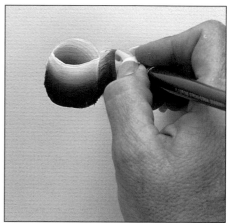

4 On the same side where the upper petal began, start on the chisel edge, with the white corner facing upward.

5 Push down lightly on the bristles and stroke your brush in a gentle "U" shape, with the white always facing upward.

6 Finish the stroke by lifting the brush to its chisel edge.

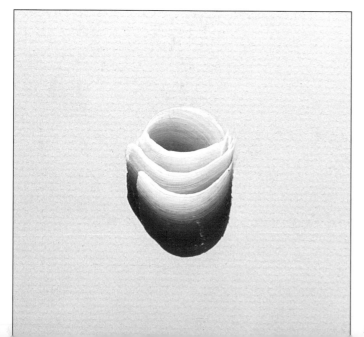

7 Repeat this U-shaped stroke two more times to give a layered look to the rosebud. Notice that the white edge is always at the top.

The Wrong Way to Make a Rosebud!

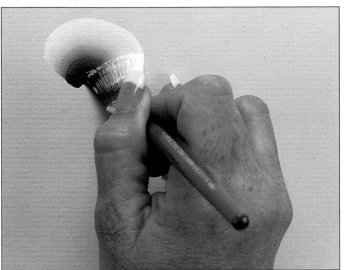

Turning the brush in a half-circle causes the white edge to face sideways in a fan shape.

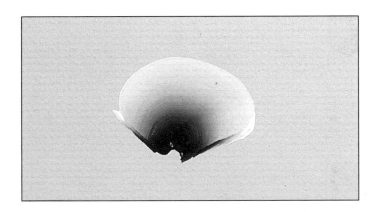

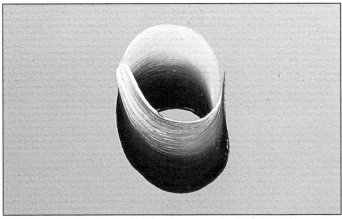

Don't leave a hole in the middle of your rosebud. If this is happening to you: (1) You may not be pushing down on the brush hard enough on the upper petal; (2) You may not be starting the lower petal in the right place; or (3) You may be exaggerating the "U" shape of the lower petal too much.

Adding the Calyx and Stem

Calyx

1 Double load a no. 12 flat brush with Wicker White and Green Forest. Start at the base of the rosebud on the chisel edge of the brush.

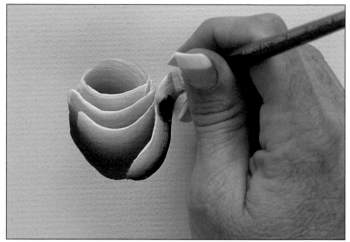

2 Push down on the bristles and stroke upward, leading with the white edge.

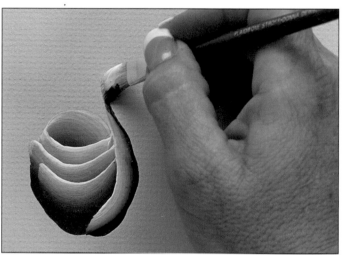

3 Follow around the shape of the rosebud, then lift the brush at the point of the calyx.

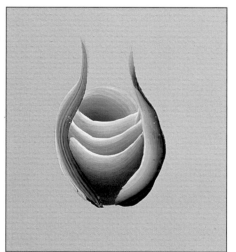

4 Repeat on the other side of the bud, leaving a small space at the bottom.

Stem

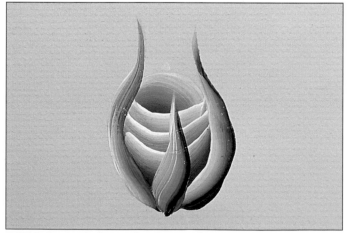

5 With the chisel edge, push a short stroke up the center of the bud.

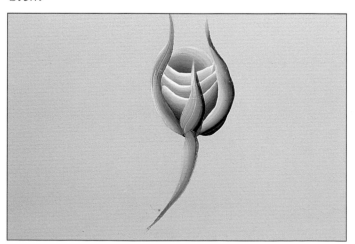

Add the stem, stroking downward from the base of the bud.

How to Paint a Shell Stroke

1 Shell strokes are an easy way to make lush cabbage roses. What's the secret to making a beautiful shell stroke? Be sure your brush is fully loaded! (If you need to, review the steps for correctly loading your brush on pages 18-23.) Begin by double loading a ¾-inch (1.9cm) flat brush with Wicker White and Berry Wine. Start on the chisel edge with the white facing upward. Push down on the bristles.

2 Make M-shaped motions with your brush, keeping your eyes on the white corner of the brush.

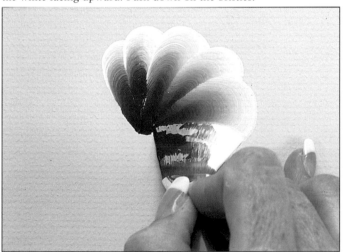

3 Pivot the Berry Wine corner of the brush as you continue to make M-shaped motions with the brush.

4 Slide on the chisel edge to finish the stroke.

5 There you have it—a beautiful cabbage rose petal in five seconds flat! Practice making your motions fluid and graceful, and be sure your brush is properly loaded so you don't run out of paint in the middle of the stroke.

How to Paint C-Stroke Petals

Closed C-Stroke

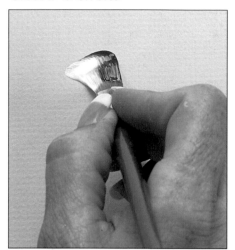 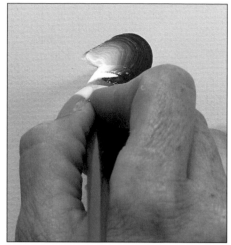 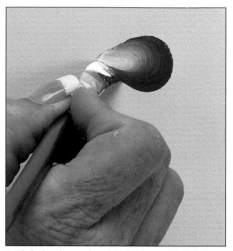

1 Double load a no. 12 flat brush with Wicker White and Dioxazine Purple. Starting on the chisel edge, push down on the bristles.

2 Shove the bristles up, making the bristles do the work.

3 Slide back on the chisel edge to finish the stroke.

Open C-Stroke

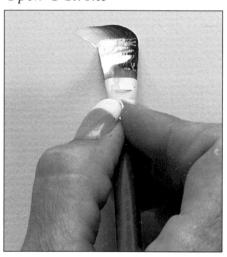

1 Double load a no. 12 flat brush with Wicker White and Dioxazine Purple. Starting on the chisel edge, push down on the bristles.

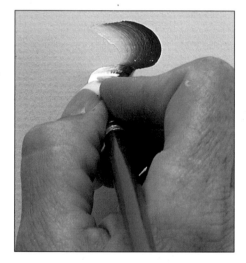

2 Stroke the brush in a "C" shape.

Layered C-Stroke Petals

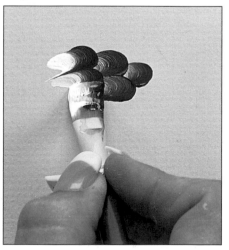 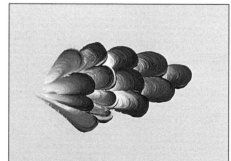

Make layers of your C-strokes from right to left.

How to Paint Leaves

Basic Leaf

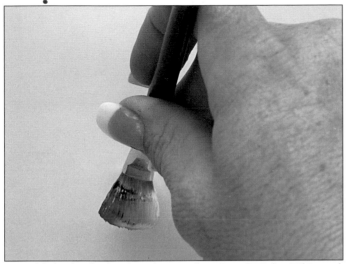

1 Double load a flat brush with two colors. I used Wicker White and Green Forest here. Starting on the chisel edge, push down on the bristles.

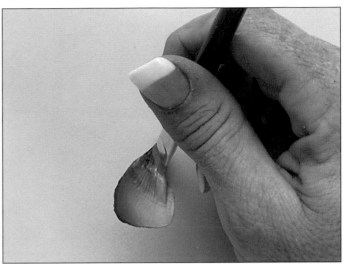

2 Now turn the green corner of the brush toward the tip of the leaf.

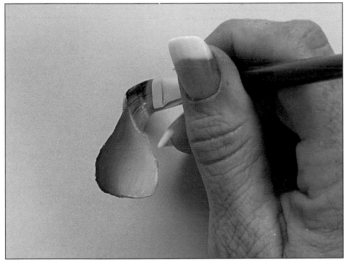

3 To bring the leaf to a point, lift the brush to its chisel edge.

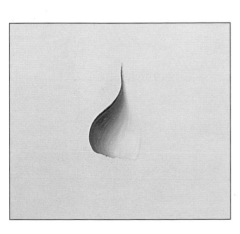

4 This is how your One-Stroke leaves should look.

5 To connect the leaves, pull the stem into the leaves to make a vine.

Scallop-Edged Leaf

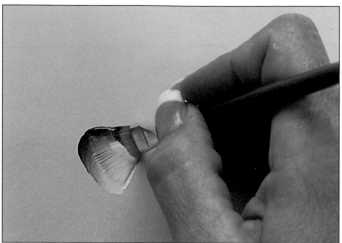

1 Double load a ¾-inch (1.9cm) flat brush with two colors. Green Forest and Sunflower are shown here.

2 Starting on the chisel edge, push the bristles down and make an M-shaped motion with your brush. Keep your eyes on the green corner of the brush.

3 Stop making the "M" motion at this point.

4 Lift the brush to its chisel edge.

5 To paint the other half of the leaf, start on the chisel edge with the yellow corner of the brush facing toward the tip of the leaf. Push down on the bristles.

6 Slide across the leaf, lifting the brush to its chisel edge at the tip of the leaf.

7 Pull the stem into the center of the leaf, leading with the yellow corner of the brush.

This shape should form a "V" at the top

Start your chisel edge at each line of the "V"

1 When both halves of the leaf are together, the leaf should be shaped like a heart, with the green on the outside all the way to the tip.

2 Pull the stem into the center of the leaf, leading with the yellow corner of the brush.

~ Donna's Hints ~

Compare the shapes of these two leaves. The one on the right is painted incorrectly—the leaf shape is too elongated. To fix this, as you're making the "M" motion with your brush, pivot the inside (yellow) corner of the brush.

One-Stroke Fruit Leaf

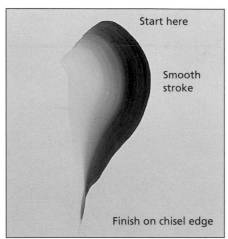

Start here

Smooth stroke

Finish on chisel edge

1 Double load a ¾-inch (1.9cm) flat brush with Green Forest and School Bus Yellow. Paint half of the leaf with one smooth stroke from base to tip.

2 Repeat step 1 for the other half of the leaf.

3 With the chisel edge, pull the stem into the leaf.

All-In-One Leaf With Stem

1 Double load a ¾-inch (1.9cm) flat brush with Green Forest and School Bus Yellow. Paint a basic One-Stroke leaf, lifting the brush to its chisel edge at the leaf's tip. Don't lift your brush off the surface.

2 Drag the brush on its chisel edge back toward the starting point of the leaf.

3 Without lifting the brush off the surface, continue through the center of the leaf to form a stem.

4 You can also paint an all-in-one leaf with a scalloped edge by following the same steps.

Ivy Leaf

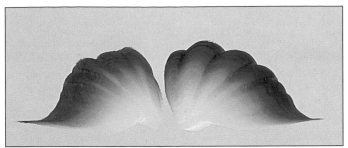

1 Double load a ¾-inch (1.9cm) flat brush with Green Forest and School Bus Yellow. Paint two scallop-edged half-leaves to form "angel wings."

2 Paint one-half of a heart-shaped leaf below one of the angel wings.

3 Paint the other half of the heart-shaped leaf under the other wing.

4 With the chisel edge, pull the stem into the center of the leaf.

Super-Easy "Slide" Leaves

1 Double load any size flat brush. Starting on the chisel edge, slide the brush at a slight angle with the green corner toward the leaf tip.

2 Paint light, airy chisel-edged strokes into the leaves to form grassy stems.

Sunflower Leaf

1 A sunflower leaf has a more exaggerated M-shaped stroke than a scallop-edged leaf, but the technique of painting it is about the same. First, double load a ¾-inch (1.9cm) flat brush with Green Forest and School Bus Yellow. Keep the green corner of the brush to the outside edge.

2 Watch the green edge as you pivot the yellow corner of the brush to form the exaggerated "M" shapes.

3 Maintain the exaggerated "M" motion all the way to the tip of the leaf, lifting the brush to its chisel edge for the final stroke.

4 Repeat steps 1 through 3 for the other half of the leaf. Remember to keep the green to the outside edge of the leaf.

5 Pull a stem into the center of the leaf, leading with the lighter color.

Turned-Edge Leaf

1 Since not all leaves lie perfectly flat in nature, here's an easy way to add interest to a leaf by giving it a turned-over edge. Start with a double-loaded ¾-inch (1.9cm) flat brush and paint one-half of a scallop-edged leaf. Pull the stem into the leaf.

2 Repeat step 1 to paint the other half of the scallop-edged leaf.

3 Now stand the brush on its chisel edge and begin to flip the brush.

4 Flip the brush completely, turning the green back toward the tip of the leaf.

5 Lift the brush to its chisel edge and slide it out to the tip of the leaf.

6 Here's the finished turned-edge leaf!

~ Practicing Your Strokework ~

1. To help you understand and practice your strokes, place a piece of clear acetate over my brushstrokes in this book, and paint on the acetate. Make sure you are pushing down on the brush bristles as hard as I am and lifting your brush when I lift mine.

2. Pull your acetate off to check your results. Acetate can be wiped clean with a damp cloth as long as the paint is still wet.

How to Paint Branches and Grapevines

Branches

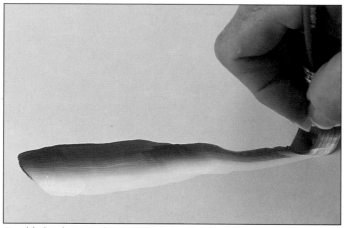 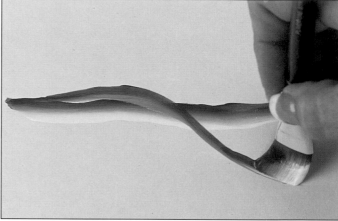

Double load a ¾-inch (1.9cm) flat brush with Wicker White and Maple Syrup. Starting on the chisel edge, push down on the bristles. Turn the brush slightly as you stroke downward, leading with the white edge. Wiggle the brush slightly following the pattern to make a more natural-looking branch. Taper off to a point by lifting the brush to its chisel edge. To add smaller branches, start on the chisel edge and lead with the white edge.

Grapevines

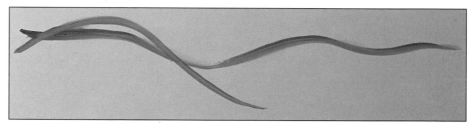

2 Start on one side of the vine and stroke across, leading with the white edge. Cross back and forth over the first vine.

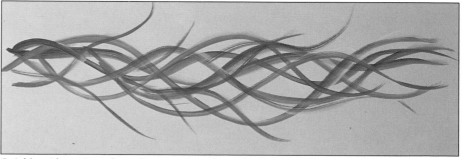

1 Double load a no. 12 flat brush with Wicker White and Maple Syrup. Starting on the chisel edge and leading with the white edge of the brush, stroke the first vine with an easy, curving motion.

3 Add random vines along the grapevine, always leading with the white edge. Vary the stroke lengths and keep your brush motion gently curving.

How to Paint Vines, Grass and Curlicues

Leafy Vines

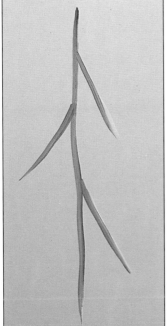

Wrong! Don't paint just one straight vine with evenly spaced sticks coming off; it looks stiff and unnatural.

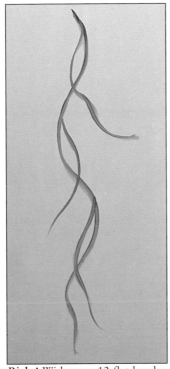

Right! With a no. 12 flat brush, start on the chisel edge and lead with the lighter color. Trail the vines from one side to the other for a more natural, flowing look.

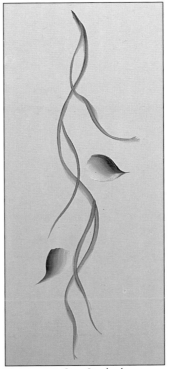

Paint some One-Stroke leaves slightly away from the vine, not right on it.

Paint connecting stems from the vine into the leaves.

Grass

1 Using a double-loaded flat brush, stroke upward on the chisel edge, leading with the lighter color.

2 Lift off of the chisel edge to form the pointy tips of the grass blades. Fill in with light, airy strokes of random lengths.

Curlicues

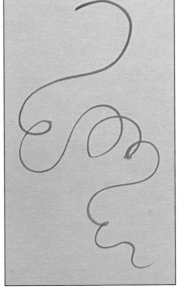

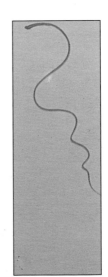

Curlicues can be done two ways: (1) curl the stroke one way, then reverse its direction back and forth (left); or (2) wiggle the stroke out from its starting point (right). I use a script liner loaded with inky-consistency paint.

Pouncing and Sponging

1 Double load a scruffy brush with Dioxazine Purple and Wicker White. Hold the brush straight up in your hand. Move your *hand* around in a pouncing motion, but don't turn the brush in your hand. Always keep the same color at the top.

2 To form wisteria, lean your scruffy brush on its edge and trail off with a lighter pouncing motion, still keeping the same color at the top.

3 Taper off gently to the tip of the wisteria.

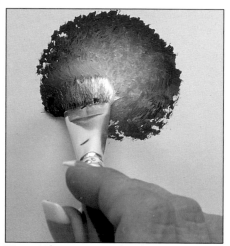

Wrong! If you turn your brush as you're pouncing, you will get a donut-looking shape. If your pouncing motion is correct, you'll! have highlights and shadings, *and* the proper shape!

Wrong! If you load Butter Pecan on your sponge and pounce it (above left), and then come back and load white on your sponge and pounce it (above right), the colors are too separated, and the result looks stark and hard edged.

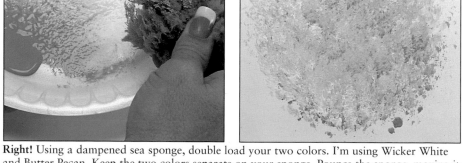

Right! Using a dampened sea sponge, double load your two colors. I'm using Wicker White and Butter Pecan. Keep the two colors separate on your sponge. Pounce the sponge, moving it randomly over the surface. Try not to create a regular pattern. Reload your sponge as needed, but keep the colors separate.

How to Paint Bows and Ribbons

Double-Loaded Bow

1 Double load a no. 12 flat brush. I'm using Midnight and Wicker White. Starting on the chisel edge, push down on the bristles and start your first loop.

2 Continue the loop, gradually lifting the brush to its chisel edge.

3 Bring the loop back to the center. Notice that the white corner of the brush is still on the same side.

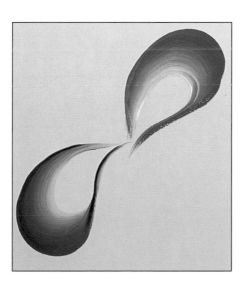

4 For the second loop, turn your brush over so the white corner is on the other side, and make a loop just as you did in steps 1 through 3.

Double-Loaded Ribbon

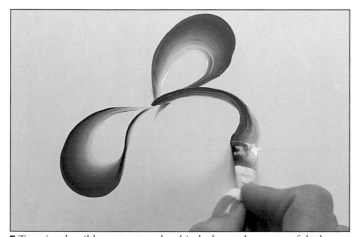

5 To paint the ribbon, start on the chisel edge at the center of the loops.

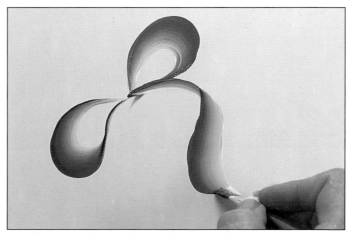

6 Push down on the bristles to widen the stroke and to shade one side of the ribbon, and then lift the brush to its chisel edge.

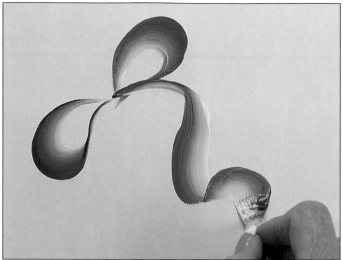

7 Flip the brush completely over as you push down on the bristles, and then lift the brush to its chisel edge. Now the shaded edge is on the other side of the ribbon. Continue with this motion to make more curls in the ribbon.

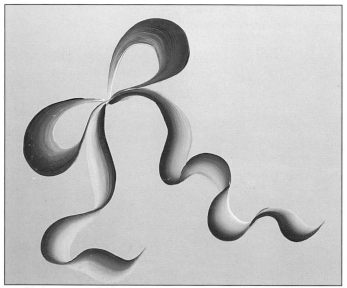

8 Add the second ribbon, varying the shape of the curls. To bring the ends of the ribbons to a nice, neat point, just lift your brush to its chisel edge.

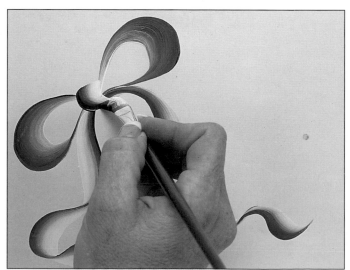

9 Paint an open C-stroke to tie the center together.

String Bow

1 Using a no. 2 script liner with inky-consistency paint, paint each loop as a separate stroke.

2 Add two ribbons coming from the center of each loop.

3 Tie the bow in the middle with three little C-strokes. Highlight with white in the center of the bow.

Watercolor Shading

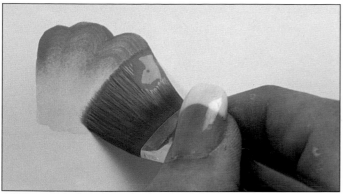

1 Using a ¾-inch (1.9cm) flat brush side loaded with Butter Pecan, make a One-Stroke scallop-edged leaf. (Turn to page 23 if you are unsure how to side load your brush.)

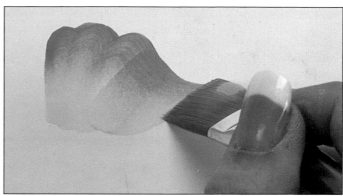

2 Lift to the chisel edge at the tip of the leaf.

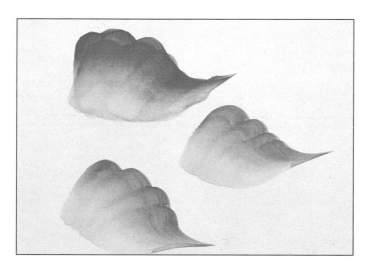

3 Repeat steps 1 and 2 for a cluster of three leaves.

4 Paint stems into each leaf with the chisel edge of the brush. I used this watercolor shading technique to paint the subtle leaves and vines on the outside edges of the Fruit Cabinet (see page 107).

Watercolor Shadowing

1 Here's a finished plum similar to the one shown on page 110. Let's give it a more realistic look by adding shadows underneath the plum and the leaf.

2 Side load a no. 12 flat brush with Maple Syrup and stroke along the lower edge of the plum. Keep the Maple Syrup corner of the brush next to the fruit.

3 Create a shadow in the same manner underneath the leaf. Just stroke across the face of the plum, keeping the Maple Syrup corner next to the leaf.

Antiquing

1 The Ivy Keepsake Box project on pages 70-77 will give you an opportunity to add a little antiquing to your basecoated surface. The antiquing is done first, before you transfer the pattern. Shown here is the oval bentwood box and lid as it comes from the store. First, fill any holes with wood filler, and then lightly sand the surface and clean off the dust.

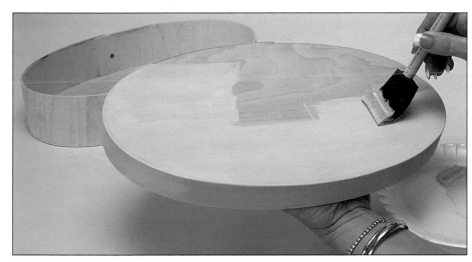

2 With a sponge applicator, basecoat the surface (I'm using Sunflower) in the direction of the grain. Lightly sand, and then apply another coat. Let dry.

3 Dampen a clean household sponge and squeeze out excess water.

4 Lightly brush just the edge of the dampened sponge into the antiquing color (Harvest Gold).

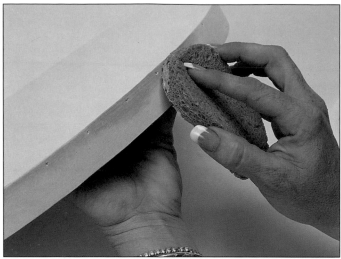

5 Apply the antiquing color all the way around the edge of the lid.

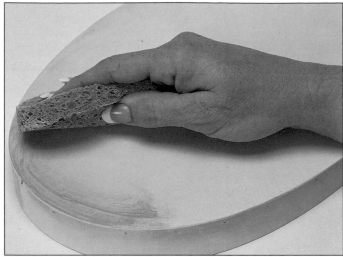

6 Rub the antiquing color around the top edge of the lid.

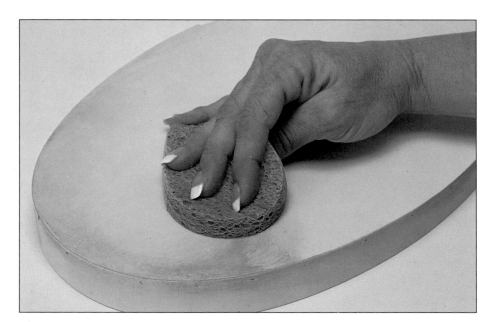

7 Pull the color in a circular motion toward the center of the lid.

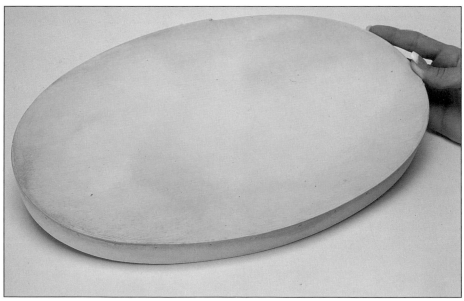

8 The result should be a natural-looking, aged effect with random light and dark shadings.

Tracing the Pattern

1 Lay a piece of tracing paper over the original drawing or pattern.

2 Trace the outer shape of each leaf and flower, ignoring the small details.

3 Insert a piece of graphite paper, dark side down, underneath the tracing paper. Using a stylus, trace the pattern onto the basecoated and antiqued surface. (Don't trace curlicues; it makes the pattern more difficult to paint.)

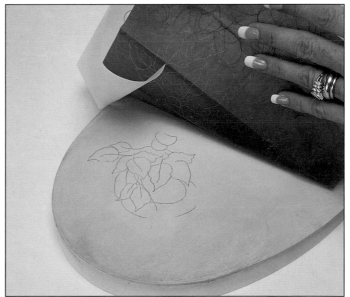

4 Lift your paper occasionally to check your progress. Hold the pattern in place with your other hand so the design doesn't shift. When the drawing has been completely transferred, begin painting the flowers and leaves on top of the antiqued surface.

Garden Birdhouse Mailbox

Every day we go to our mailboxes to collect our mail. Sometimes we receive good news and sometimes nothing more than a stack of bills. Nevertheless, that trip to the mailbox is a daily ritual. I decided to make it a more enjoyable one, and what better way than to create a beautifully painted mailbox to greet you each day! The mailbox I used is a standard rural type, but the One-Stroke technique can be adapted to any type of mailbox. Once you master this technique, you'll probably be painting all kinds of surfaces.

One thing to remember is that painting is supposed to be fun. When in doubt or under stress, take a deep breath and lighten up! I taught myself to paint by practicing in the evenings, after a long day of mothering my seven children. Painting was—and is—a way to relieve stress, not cause it!

~ Donna's Hints ~

- Don't use water except when painting the curlicues.

- Remember—if there is not enough paint in the brushes you won't be able to achieve the One-Stroke technique, so don't be afraid to load up that brush!

- If you do overload the brush, simply wipe some paint off with paper towels. (If you clean the brush with water, you will need to wipe the brush dry before reloading it.)

- Pay close attention to the use of the flat brushes, especially when I refer to the chisel edge, or the tips of the bristles. I use the chisel edge of the brush as a starting point, a finishing point and for many steps where another brush, such as a script liner or a smaller flat brush, might be used.

~ Materials ~

Rural mailbox: It should be approximately 19″ long × 6½″ wide × 9″ high (48.3cm × 16.5cm × 22.9cm). These mailboxes are available in most local hardware and building supply stores and are usually already prepainted in a variety of colors. White, the most common color, is what I've chosen for this project.

Brushes: You'll need a ¾-inch (1.9cm) flat brush, a no. 12 flat brush, a no. 2 script liner and my favorite, a scruffy brush. I recommend the FolkArt One-Stroke Brushes by Plaid, which come packaged in a three-piece set. The flat brushes of gold nylon have an exceptional chisel edge, which is an important factor in painting with this technique. The scruffy brush is made of natural bristles and is sold individu-

ally. I know many painters have a number of scruffy brushes, but I think if you try my scruffy brush, you'll see what a difference it makes. My scruffy brush has unique features—the oval shape, the spring of the bristles and the overall uniformity—that are uncommon to most scruffy brushes.

Spray lacquer: Use a good quality lacquer with a good spray tip. It's best to apply two or three light coats and build up to the desired finish in steps rather than apply the finish in one heavy coat.

Good quality acrylic paints: I use the FolkArt Acrylic Colors by Plaid. The colors needed for this project are shown below.

#448 Green Forest

#434 Berry Wine

#901 Wicker White

#763 School Bus Yellow

#945 Maple Syrup

#443 Night Sky

#558 Dioxazine Purple

#939 Butter Pecan

The Garden Bird-
house Mailbox pat-
tern on pages 54-55
may be hand-traced
or photocopied for
personal use only.
Enlarge at 118% to
return the image to
full size.

Paint the Birdhouses

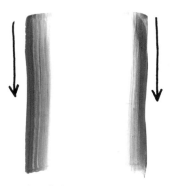

Body of Shingled Birdhouse

Double load a ¾-inch (1.9cm) flat brush with Wicker White and Maple Syrup. Stroke down with the Maple Syrup on the outside edge. Stroke both sides of the birdhouse.

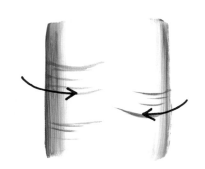

Rounding the Birdhouse

While the body paint is still wet, use the no. 2 script liner, with light pressure, to pull paint from the edges toward the center of the birdhouse. This will give it a rounded look.

Birdhouse Base

Load a no. 12 flat brush with Night Sky and use the chisel edge to paint the base in one motion. The brush will need to be loaded properly so you can achieve this stroke in one fluid motion.

Birdhouse Hole and Perch

Dip the end of the handle on the no. 2 script liner into the Maple Syrup and dot the hole. Load the no. 2 script liner with Maple Syrup and, using the tip of the brush, paint the perch. Load the no. 2 script liner with Wicker White, and paint the highlights on the holes and the perch with a light touch of the tip of the brush.

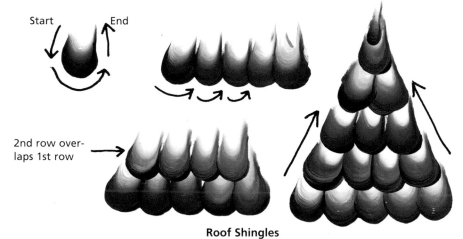

Roof Shingles

Load the no. 12 flat brush with Wicker White and Berry Wine. With the Berry Wine to the outside edge, start on the chisel edge of the brush and paint downward, laying the brush down to form the bottom of the shingle. As you come up, lift the brush to its chisel edge. Repeat for each shingle until a row is formed. Start with the lowest row, making sure the lowest row of shingles overlaps the top edge of the birdhouse.

Paint the next row of shingles, overlapping the lower row. Form slightly smaller shingles as you paint upwards, and decrease the number of shingles in each row.

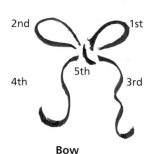

Bow

Load a no. 2 script liner with Night Sky and use the tip of the brush to paint the bow in light, short strokes in the order shown. I like to rest my pinky finger against the surface I'm painting; it serves as a guide and steadies my hand as I make these strokes.

Finished Birdhouse

We'll add the pole and the twining foliage later (see page 59).

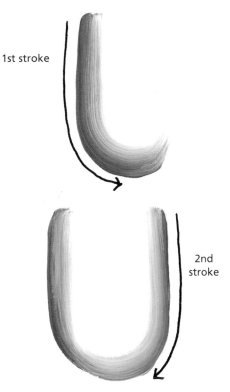

1st stroke

2nd stroke

Mossy Birdhouse

Double load a no. 12 flat brush with Wicker White and Maple Syrup. With the Maple Syrup to the outside edge, pull each side down to the base and lift the brush to finish the stroke.

Moss on Top of Birdhouse

Load your scruffy brush with Wicker White and Green Forest, and pounce straight up and down on the top of the birdhouse to form a large mound of moss. Remember not to pounce too hard or you might "muddy up" the moss. Keep the colors separate on the scruffy brush to achieve the variations in color.

Paint the hole and perch the same way you did on the first birdhouse.

Add Wisteria

After the moss has dried, load the scruffy brush with Dioxazine Purple and Wicker White, and pounce lightly over the moss to form wisteria. On the next two pages you'll learn how to paint the pole and the leaves.

Paint the Leaves, Grass and Tendrils

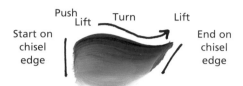

One-Stroke Leaves

Double load a no. 12 flat brush with Wicker White and Green Forest. Starting the brush on its chisel edge, push downward, turn the brush and lift it to its chisel edge, lifting to the tip of the leaf. Remember: three steps—push, turn and lift.

One-Stroke Leaves With Stems

Paint One-Stroke leaves the same as before. To paint a stem, use the chisel edge of the no. 12 flat brush and pull into the leaf.

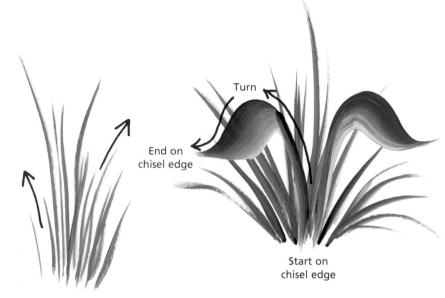

Grass

Double load a no. 12 flat brush with Wicker White and Green Forest. Paint short, upward strokes, leading with Wicker White, and drag the bristles to end the grass blades. For a natural look, make sure that the grass spreads out at the top and that each blade is broader at its base.

Broadleaf Grass Blades

With a no. 12 flat brush double loaded with Wicker White and Green Forest, start on the chisel edge of the brush and make an upward stroke. Now lay down the brush, pull downward and then lift the brush to its chisel edge.

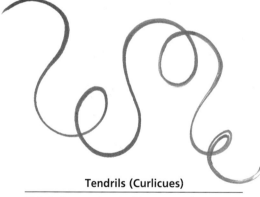

Tendrils (Curlicues)

This is the one time I add water to the paint! With a no. 2 script liner, add a small amount of water to the Green Forest paint to make an inky consistency. Load the brush with the inky paint, and remove the excess by rolling the brush until it's loaded but not dripping. Now paint the curlicues using the tip of the brush.

～ Donna's Hints ～

When I first started to paint, one of the most difficult things I encountered was painting curlicues. I discovered that if I braced my pinky finger against the paper, I could steady the brush and guide the stroke. Curlicues and tendrils are a lot easier now!

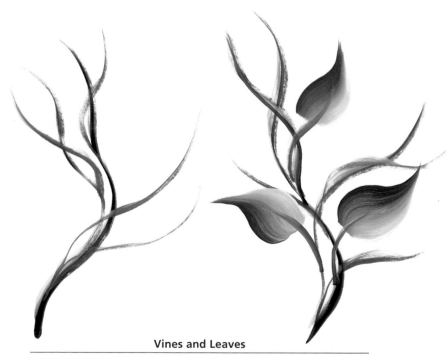

Vines and Leaves

Double load a no. 12 flat brush with Wicker White and Green Forest. Paint the vines using the chisel edge of the brush, making sure to lead with the white edge. Now you can paint the One-Stroke leaves onto the vines.

Paint the Pole and Moss

1st layer

2nd layer

Grass and Moss

Double load the scruffy brush with Wicker White and Green Forest. Pounce the scruffy brush straight up and down to form the grass and moss. Be sure to keep the colors separate so they don't get muddy. Taper the ends of the moss to create a more natural appearance. Remember to keep the Green Forest to the outside edge.

Birdhouse Pole

Double load a no. 12 flat brush with Wicker White and Maple Syrup. Using the chisel edge of the brush, paint the pole with a downward stroke. You may lead with either color. Allow the pole to dry before proceeding.

Weaving the Moss up the Pole

Double load the scruffy brush with Wicker White and Green Forest. Pounce the brush upward, starting from the bottom of the pole and twisting around the pole to the top. Remember to leave spaces for the pole to show through.

Paint the Flowers

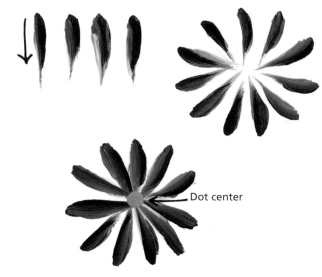

Narrow-Petal Flowers

Double load a no. 12 flat brush with Berry
Wine and Wicker White. Using the chisel edge
of the brush, stroke towards the center of the
flower. Dot the center with School Bus Yellow
using the wooden tip of the brush.

Blue Flowers

Double load a no. 12 flat brush with Wicker
White and Night Sky. Using the chisel edge of
the brush, paint upward, then pull down and
back onto the chisel edge. Repeat this stroke to
form all the petals of the flower.

Using the handle end of the no. 12 flat
brush, dot the center of the flower with School
Bus Yellow.

Note: The trailing flowers need to become
smaller as you paint away from the full flowers.

Stalk Flowers

Double load a no. 12 flat brush with Wicker
White and Night Sky. Paint the petals with the
chisel edge of the brush. Begin at the top and
paint downward, layering the petals to form
the tapered shape of the stalk. Stalk flowers can
be painted with other colors, too.

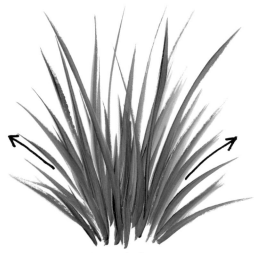

Grass Blades

Double load a no. 12 flat brush with Wicker
White and Green Forest. Using the chisel edge
of the brush, make short upward strokes, lifting
the brush to its tip to create the pointed ends of
the grass blades. Paint areas of grass blades to
fill in between the stalk flowers. Allow to dry.

Watering Can and Clay Pots

When I first began my painting career I needed a lot of practice, and surfaces to paint on were sometimes expensive. In my search for an inexpensive surface I discovered clay pots, and a whole new world opened up for me. This was a surface I could paint for a reasonable cost. No matter how awful my painting, the plants I put in the pots always seemed to make them beautiful. I basecoated the clay pots and painted everything from roses to sunflowers on them. I gave many of them as gifts, sometimes with a lot of foliage draping over the sides to conceal my painting. Others were filled with homemade rolls and muffins. Clay pots come in an array of sizes and shapes, so the possibilities are endless.

The watering can complements the clay pots and is a beautiful accent piece. It is functional as well, allowing you to water the plants in the clay pots.

I chose the wildflowers as a tribute to my mother-in-law, who loved wildflowers in her yard.

~ Donna's Hints ~

It is important to basecoat and seal the inside of the pot, as well as the outside. Basecoat the flower pots with Tapioca #903.

~ Materials ~

Clay pots: Use two standard pots, approximately 6″ and 7″ (15cm and 18cm) in size. These are available at any hardware or garden supply store.

Watering can: It should be enamel coated, approximately 8″ in diameter × 9″ high (20cm × 23cm), and should have a shower spout and curved neck. I found this one through a local garden supply store.

Brushes: I used a ¾-inch (1.9cm) flat brush, a no. 12 flat brush, a no. 2 script liner and a scruffy brush.

Sponge brush: Use a 2-inch (5cm) sponge brush to basecoat the pots.

Sealer: Use #789 FolkArt Acrylic Sealer matte finish or #787 FolkArt Clearcote Glaze gloss finish, depending on your preference.

Good quality acrylic paints: I used FolkArt Acrylic Colors by Plaid. The colors needed for this project are shown below.

#558 Dioxazine Purple

#434 Berry Wine

#917 Harvest Gold

#432 Sunflower

#945 Maple Syrup

#448 Green Forest

#901 Wicker White

This pattern may be hand-traced or photocopied for personal use only. Enlarge at 154% to return the image to full size.

This pattern may be hand-traced or photocopied for personal use only.

Paint the Daisy

Moss

Multi-load a scruffy brush with Green Forest, Sunflower and Wicker White. Make sure these colors are loaded in separate areas of the brush and not mixed together.

Pounce the scruffy brush straight up and down to create the moss on the clay pots or the watering can. It is important not to mix the colors in a swirling motion. This will not give the moss depth or texture.

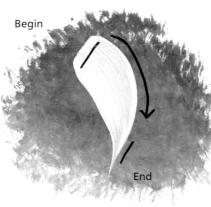

Daisy Petals

Load a no. 12 flat brush with Wicker White.

Begin on the chisel edge and push down as you slide the brush upwards, lifting it to its chisel edge and sliding it into the previously painted centers. Repeat the stroke.

Paint the petals around the center to form the flower.

Center of Daisy Flower

Load a scruffy brush with Maple Syrup and Harvest Gold.

Once again, pounce the brush up and down to form the center of each flower.

Flower Center

Repounce the center to define it clearly.

Paint the Small Pink Daisies

Double load a no. 12 flat brush with Wicker White and Berry Wine.

    With the chisel edge facing downward, lead with the white edge. Stand the brush on its chisel edge and push slightly as you slide towards the center of the flower.

Repeat the stroke to place additional petals around the perimeter, always touching the center.

Form a circle.

Finished small pink daisy.

Paint the Vines and Leaves

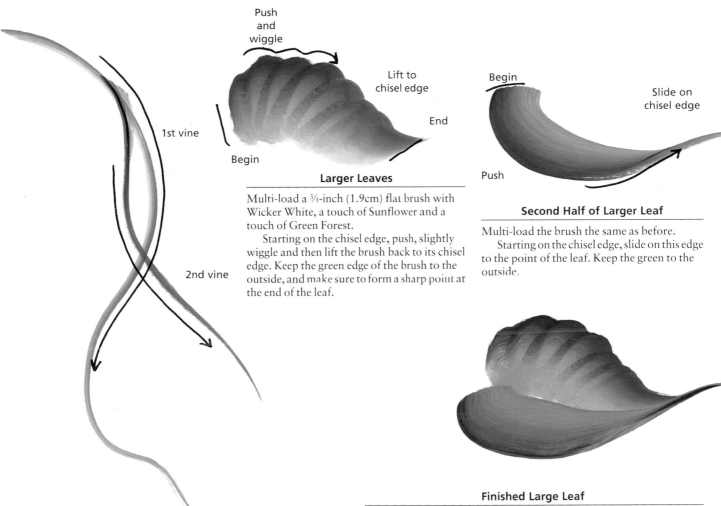

Push and wiggle

Lift to chisel edge

1st vine

Begin

End

2nd vine

Begin

Slide on chisel edge

Push

Larger Leaves

Multi-load a ¾-inch (1.9cm) flat brush with Wicker White, a touch of Sunflower and a touch of Green Forest.

Starting on the chisel edge, push, slightly wiggle and then lift the brush back to its chisel edge. Keep the green edge of the brush to the outside, and make sure to form a sharp point at the end of the leaf.

Second Half of Larger Leaf

Multi-load the brush the same as before.

Starting on the chisel edge, slide on this edge to the point of the leaf. Keep the green to the outside.

Finished Large Leaf

Notice the sharp point of the leaf.

Double load a no. 12 flat brush with Wicker White and Green Forest.

Paint the vines using the chisel edge of the brush, leading with the white edge. The vines should be coming out from the flower clusters and twining around the project. Interlace the vines as you paint them.

Leaf Stem

Double load a ¾-inch (1.9cm) flat brush with Wicker White and Green Forest.

Start on the chisel edge and paint the stems into the leaf, leading with the white edge.

～ One-Stroke Leaves ～

Multi-load a no. 12 flat brush with Wicker White, Green Forest and a touch of Sunflower.

Refer to chapter three for directions on these leaves.

Paint Wisteria and Small Yellow Flowers

Wisteria

Load a scruffy brush with Wicker White on one side and Pure Pigment Dioxazine Purple on the other.

Pounce straight up and down, making certain you do not twist the brush in your hand. Pounce lightly but firmly, moving your hand around and placing the wisteria where you want it.

To form the tail of the wisteria, lay the brush on its edge and pounce the tapered end of the wisteria.

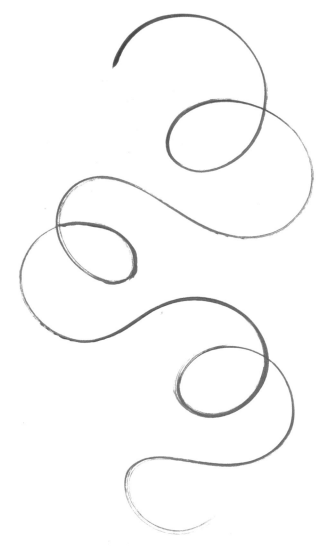

Tendrils (Curlicues)

Refer to chapter one, page 58 for directions.

Small Yellow Flower

Load a no. 12 flat brush with Sunflower. Push lightly, lifting with small, short strokes to form the petals.

Combined Petals

Once you have combined the petals, load a scruffy brush with Maple Syrup and Harvest Gold and pounce a dab in the center of the flower.

Finish the Project

This is how your finished watering can should look.

The top of the watering can.

The side view of the watering can.

This is how your finished flower pots should look.

Ivy Keepsake Box

There are some things you cannot improve upon. I think ivy falls into that category. Ivy can be managed, or it can grow wild—its beauty isn't the least bit changed. Ivy grows in all climates. It grows in our yards as well as in the deep woods.

When I am painting, I use ivy in the same way I would use it in landscaping—to fill in, to embellish and to stand alone on painted pieces. I painted this keepsake box to have a place for all the special things I have saved through the years. The box seemed to be just the right surface for the ivy.

Once you have mastered the art of painting ivy, you will be ready for all kinds of projects. If you follow my techniques, you will see just how stress-free ivy painting can be.

~ Materials ~

Bentwood box: It should be an oval box approximately 16″ in diameter × 6″ high (40cm × 15cm). The box I used was constructed of birch wood. Fasteners from a nail gun were used to hold the box together. They were countersunk, so I had to fill the holes with wood filler first. Be careful not to overfill them, because they will require sanding to smooth them out in preparation for basecoating.

Brushes: You will need a no. 12 flat brush and a no. 2 script liner.

Sponge: Use a flat, all-purpose household sponge approximately 3″ × 5″ (8cm × 13cm).

Transfer materials: You'll need some transfer/tracing paper and a stylus.

Sponge brush: Use a 2-inch (5cm) brush.

Sealer: Use #789 FolkArt Acrylic Sealer matte finish.

Good quality acrylic paints: I used FolkArt Acrylic Colors by Plaid. The colors needed for this project are shown below.

#432 Sunflower   #917 Harvest Gold   #448 Green Forest

#901 Wicker White   #404 Periwinkle

Pattern for box lid

Pattern for box sides

Enlarge at 152%

These patterns may
be hand-traced or
photocopied for per-
sonal use only.

Enlarge at 125%

Paint the Bow

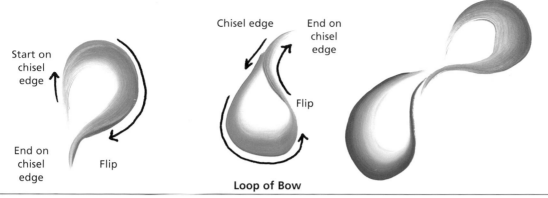

Loop of Bow

Double load a no. 12 flat brush with Wicker White and Periwinkle.

Start painting with the chisel edge, leading with the white edge. Slide the brush, then push as you turn and lift the brush to its chisel edge.

Repeat the instructions for the first loop to form the opposite loop of the bow. Loops are joined to form a bow.

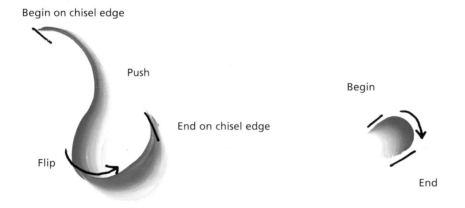

Tails on Bows

Use the same technique to paint the ribbons around the box's perimeter.

Double load the no. 12 flat brush with Wicker White and Periwinkle.

Starting on the chisel edge, slide the brush and lift it to its chisel edge to form a flip in the bow. Continue to push the brush, and lift it to its chisel edge to end the stroke.

Center of Bow

Double load the no. 12 flat brush with Wicker White and Periwinkle.

Paint the center by starting and ending on the chisel edge, with the Periwinkle to the outside. Paint both halves and end in the center to tie the loops together.

The next step is painting the ribbons around the perimeter of the box. Apply the technique you just learned. Remember to keep the brush on its chisel edge and to make light strokes so you maintain the definition of the ribbon.

Paint the Vines

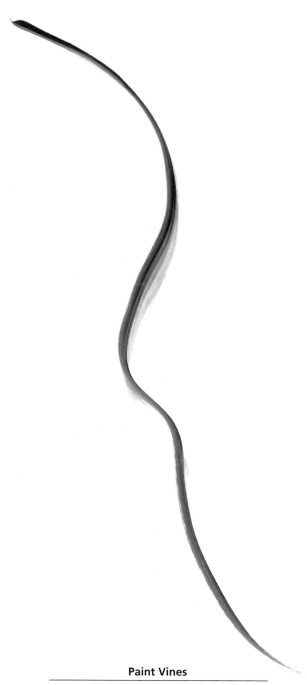

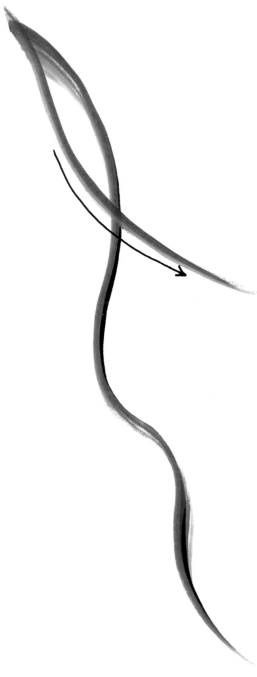

Paint Vines

Double load the no. 12 flat brush with Sunflower and Green Forest.

The vines are achieved by using the chisel edge of the brush and by leading with the lighter color. Keep the brush in an upright position as you paint. Paint the vines from the center of the bow first, and then mingle them in and out of the ribbon around the sides of the box.

Vines on Top of Vines

Load your brush as before.

The idea here is to paint vines over vines without muddying the paint. Use a weaving pattern as you cross back and forth over the other vines. Repeat this around the entire box and lid, as shown.

Paint Ivy Leaves

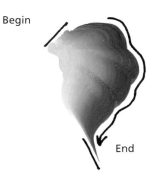

Start the Ivy Leaf

Double load the no. 12 flat brush with Sunflower and Green Forest.

When painting leaves, you will need to place them coming off the vines so you can pull the stems from the vines into the leaves.

Begin painting the leaves by starting on the chisel edge. Push and wiggle the brush slightly as you pivot the white edge. Now, stop wiggling, lift the brush to its chisel edge and slide it to the end. As you master this stroke, you will find it opens doors to a world of leaves.

When painted correctly, the leaf will look similar to an angel's wing.

Second Half of Ivy Leaf

Repeat the technique you just learned to form the second half. The leaf will now resemble a full pair of angel wings.

Center Section of Finished Ivy Leaf

Double load a no. 12 flat brush with Sunflower and Green Forest.

As you paint this part of the leaf, it will probably be helpful to picture the shape of a heart.

Paint the right side first. Stroke downward, starting and ending on the chisel edge.

Center Section of Ivy Leaf (Second Half)

Repeat the same steps to paint the left half of the leaf.

Finish the Ivy Leaf

These four strokes combine to form the finished ivy leaf.

Paint the Stems, Leaves and Curlicues

Leaf Stems

Double load a no. 12 flat brush with Sunflower and Green Forest.

Paint the stems using the chisel edge, and leading with the white. Start from the vines and lead into the leaves, lifting to the tip of the bristles as you come out of each leaf.

Tendrils (Curlicues)

Refer to chapter one, page 58.

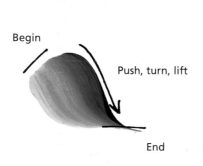

Additional Leaves

I am going to refer to these as One-Stroke leaves, because they are achieved in just that: one stroke.

Double load a no. 12 flat brush with Sunflower and Green Forest.

Painting this leaf is best explained by using the terminology "push, pull, and lift."

Starting on the chisel edge, push slightly with the green edge of the brush and pull, turning to the point of the leaf. Then lift the brush back onto the chisel edge.

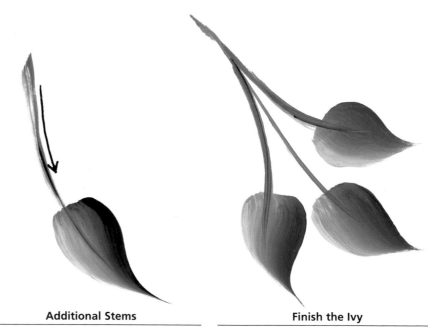

Additional Stems

Double load a no. 12 flat brush with Sunflower and Green Forest.

Using the chisel edge and leading with the white, paint the stems into the leaves.

Finish the Ivy

Paint clusters of two or more One-Stroke leaves as shown.

Finish the Project

This is how the lid of your Ivy Keepsake Box should look.

This is what the side of the box should look like.

Rosebud Memory Album

Everybody likes a personalized gift, and a hand-painted photo album is a fun and inexpensive gift to give. This album may become a cherished heirloom, full of memories that will last a lifetime. Memory albums are expensive to buy, but you can create your own and have the enjoyment of knowing it came from your heart.

⁓ Materials ⁓

Photo album or scrapbook: These can be found at most craft, discount or photo supply stores. Choose one that has a smooth cover; it will be easier to paint on than one with a textured cover. For this project, I chose a shade of lavender that would work well with the pink rosebuds and green leaves of the design.

Brushes: You will need a no. 12 flat brush and a no. 2 script liner.

Clear spray sealer: Use a good quality sealer that is compatible with the cover material.

Good quality acrylic paints: Your memory album may become a family heirloom and you'll want the colors to last, so use the best-quality paints you can find. I used FolkArt Acrylic Colors by Plaid. The colors needed for this project are shown below.

#448 Green Forest

#434 Berry Wine

#558 Dioxazine Purple

#570 Burnt Umber

#901 Wicker White

Pattern for Rosebud Memory album

This pattern may be hand-traced or photocopied for personal use only. Enlarge at 128% to return the image to full size.

Paint Lettering and Grapevines

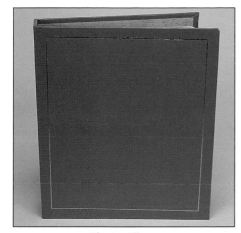

Photo Album

Purchase an inexpensive vinyl-covered photo album or scrapbook in the color of your choice.

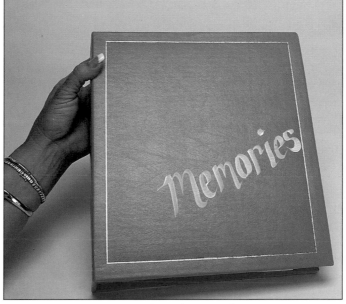

Lettering

Choose any words you like to personalize the cover. I painted the word *Memories* with a flat brush loaded with Wicker White.

Grapevines

Double load a no. 12 flat brush with Burnt Umber and Wicker White. Using the chisel edge, paint grapevines along the top left corner of the cover.

Finish the Grapevines

Embellish the grapevines as much as you want to make them fuller.

Add Bow and Ribbons

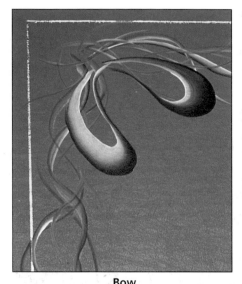

Bow

Double load a no. 12 flat brush with Dioxazine Purple and Wicker White. Paint the two loops of a shaded bow.

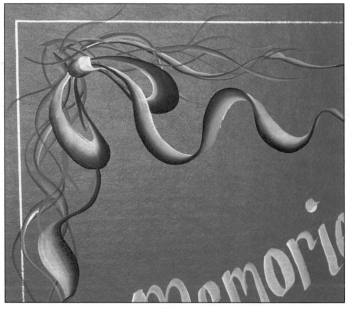

Ribbons

Add the ribbons, and then "tie" the bow in the center with a C-stroke.

Paint the Rosebuds

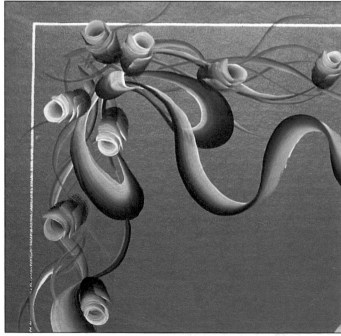

Rosebuds

Double load a no. 12 flat brush with Berry Wine and Wicker White. Paint rosebuds according to the pattern.

Calyx

Double load a no. 12 flat brush with Green Forest and Wicker White. Using the chisel edge, paint a calyx on each rosebud.

Finish With Leaves and Curlicues

Curlicues

Paint curlicues with a no. 2 script liner and inky Green Forest paint.

Leaves

Add One-Stroke leaves. Pull stems into leaves, and connect each rosebud to the vine. Sign your work with the script liner, and seal the album cover with a few light coats of clear spray sealer.

The completed Rosebud Memory Album.

Magnolia Floorcloth and Door Crown

I have always been enchanted by the beauty of the magnolia, and I still remember the first time I saw one. I was fascinated by its majestic bloom, elegant foliage and stately branches. Anyone who has witnessed the display of a blooming magnolia can tell you how captivating it is.

I was born and raised in the south. Being true to my roots, I decided to share my version of the magnolia with you. I hope I captured some of the magnolia's elegance in my painting. Hopefully, you will find a place in your heart for this grand old flower.

The floorcloth makes me feel like I am standing among magnolia blossoms, and it makes a wonderful, decorative floor covering. Maybe I'm a romantic, but I think the beauty of the magnolia will inspire you to paint.

~ Materials ~

Canvas floorcloth: It should be approximately 36″ long × 27″ wide (91cm × 69cm). The canvas for the floorcloth can be purchased in most craft and fine art supply stores and in a variety of sizes. As an alternative, you can also purchase vinyl floor covering at a building supply store. This comes in 12′ (3.7m) widths and can be cut easily with a utility knife. I paint on the reverse side of the vinyl. The preparation is the same, but you may need to apply an additional basecoat of paint. A word of caution about both of these floorcloth materials: they can be very slippery depending on where you use them, so take precautions and use an anti-slip rug pad or some other means to ensure your safety.

Brushes: I used my ¾-inch (1.9cm) flat brush and a no. 12 flat brush.

Sponge: Use a flat, all-purpose household sponge about 3″ × 5″ (8cm × 13cm).

Transfer materials: You'll need some transfer/tracing paper and a stylus.

Sealer: I used #789 FolkArt Acrylic Sealer matte finish.

Tape: Use masking or drafting tape, preferably the easy-release type.

Good quality acrylic paints: I used FolkArt Acrylic Colors by Plaid. Colors needed for this project are shown below.

#939 Butter Pecan #945 Maple Syrup #434 Berry Wine

#432 Sunflower #736 School Bus Yellow #448 Green Forest

#901 Wicker White

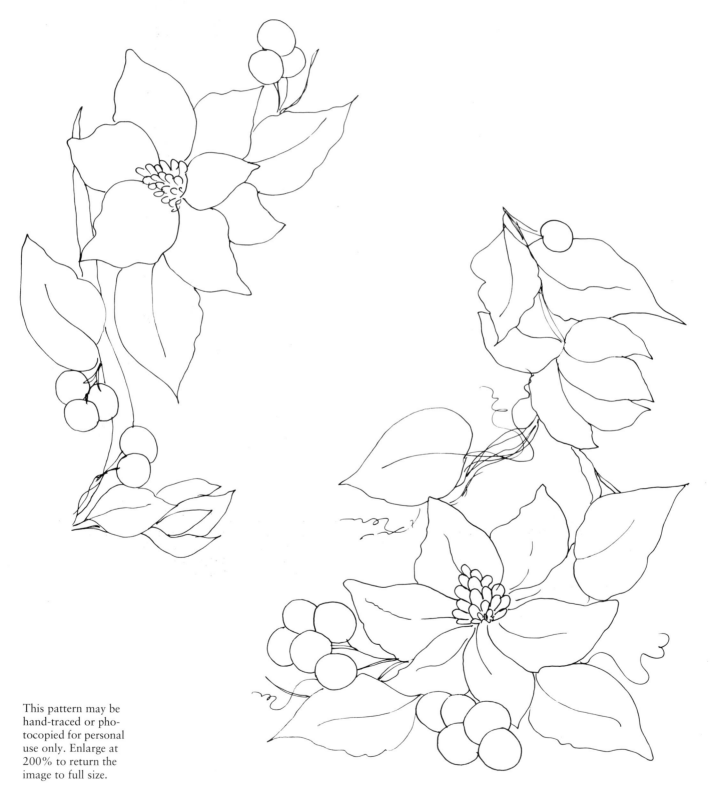

This pattern may be hand-traced or photocopied for personal use only. Enlarge at 200% to return the image to full size.

Paint the Branches

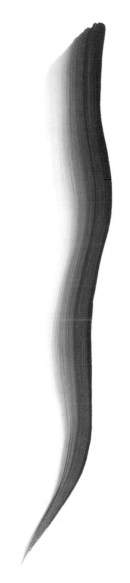

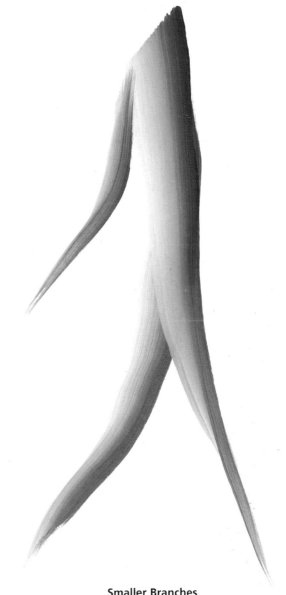

Main Branches

Double load the ¾-inch (1.9cm) flat brush with Wicker White and Maple Syrup.

Begin on the chisel edge of the brush. Push hard with the brush to form the branches. As you paint the branches, remember to lead with the white edge and to lift the brush to its chisel edge as you complete each stroke.

Smaller Branches

Start on the chisel edge at the main branch and make light strokes. Be careful to lift to the tip of the chisel edge as you complete each stroke. Once again, lead with the white edge.

Paint the Magnolia Blossoms

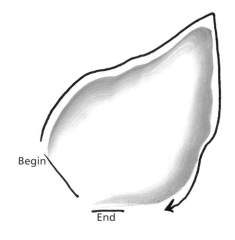

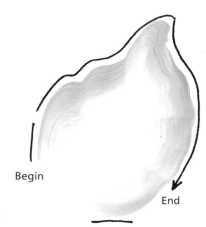

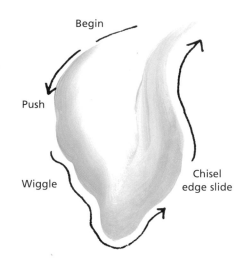

Center of Magnolia

Double load a no. 12 flat brush with School Bus Yellow and Berry Wine. Paint the center by starting at the top and making small C-strokes, painting wider rows as you go down. The small C-strokes are achieved by starting with the chisel edge on the line. Slide up and over the hill and down on the chisel edge again.

Layer C-strokes to form the center. Paint with Berry Wine to the outside edge.

Completed center.

Magnolia Flower

Combine the petals using the strokes you just learned.

I used six petals to form this flower. Layer the petals over one another as you paint. Don't worry about making an exact center, because the magnolia center will cover that area.

Pod positioning in flower.

Paint Magnolia Buds

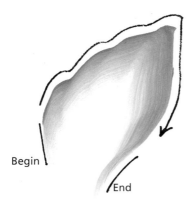

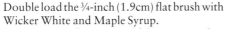

Double load the ¾-inch (1.9cm) flat brush with Wicker White and Maple Syrup.

Paint a smaller version of the same petals used in the full flower.

Paint the small closed bud by layering the petals closely over one another.

Paint the flowering buds by loading a ¾-inch (1.9cm) brush with Wicker White and Maple Syrup. Remember to begin and end on the chisel edge. Paint the petals so they form an opening bud. Allow some space between each petal, but make sure they overlap one another.

Paint Magnolia Leaves & Berries

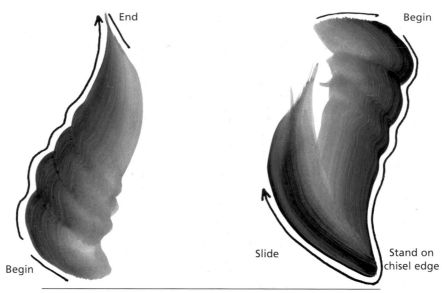

Double load the ¾-inch (1.9cm) flat brush with Green Forest and a small amount of Wicker White. Beginning on the chisel edge, push as you lightly wiggle with the green edge of the brush. Then turn up on the tip and slide as you lift the brush to its chisel edge. Do this all in one motion.

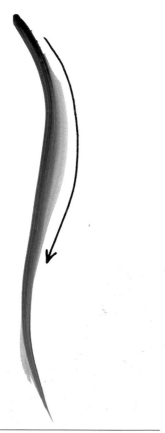

Finished Leaf

Berries

Load the ¾-inch (1.9cm) brush with the same colors as the leaves. Using the chisel edge, paint the stems. Paint from the branches about halfway into the leaf. Be sure to lightly lift the brush to its chisel edge as you finish each stroke. Remember to lead with the white edge.

Combine the two sides to form a full leaf. Fill in the leaves around the branches, around the base of each bud and around the full flowers.

Double load the no. 12 flat brush with Wicker White and Berry Wine.

Start on the chisel edge and turn the brush in a half-circle. Then start at the same spot again and paint in counterclockwise motion until the two halves meet. If the berry is rough, stroke back and forth lightly until smooth. When you paint the clumps of berries, you don't have to complete the circle on the underlying berries.

Finish the Project

Paint large magnolia flowers around the outside of the floor-cloth. Place one on each corner and one in the center of each side. This is how your finished floorcloth should look.

When painting the door crown, be sure to paint one full flower in the center of the project. This is how your completed door crown should look.

Wild Rose Birdhouse

The idea for this project came from a visit to my in-laws' home. They have a backyard full of flowers, and right in the center is a bird feeder on a post. When we visit, we always admire the numerous species of birds frequenting the feeder. I enjoy the quiet beauty of nature through these beautiful birds, and I reflect on how special the little things in life can be.

I would love to have my own bird feeder. However, we have two very inquisitive cats, so the birds would not visit much. In an attempt to satisfy my yearning to see birds, my husband designed this little indoor birdhouse and attached it to a table leg on a 12"-square (30cm-square) base. We use this birdhouse to leave messages for one another. It looks much better than a message board and even adds a decorative touch to the room. My cats enjoy it, too. Sometimes they seem to watch the birdhouse, expecting a visit from our feathered friends.

~ Materials ~

Birdhouse post: Use a turned table leg approximately 4" in diameter × 36" high (10cm × 91cm). This can be purchased at a building supply store. Remember, you don't have to purchase the exact post I did. There are many different styles available. You can also buy stair parts, such as a newel post, that will serve the same purpose. You'll also need a 1"-thick (2.5cm-thick) board, approximately 12" × 12" (30cm × 30cm), for a base.

Birdhouse: Mine is approximately 6" wide × 6" deep × 11" high (15cm × 15cm × 28cm). Any size birdhouse will work, but keep in mind that the size of the post should be in relation to the size of the birdhouse. The proportions must be correct.

Brushes: I used a ¾-inch (1.9cm) flat brush, a no. 12 flat brush, a no. 2 script liner and a scruffy brush.

Transfer materials: You'll need some tracing/transfer paper and a stylus.

Sponge brush: Use a 2-inch (5cm) foam sponge brush for basecoating.

Sealer: I used #789 FolkArt Acrylic Sealer matte finish.

Good quality acrylic paints: I used FolkArt Acrylic Colors by Plaid. Colors needed for this project are shown below.

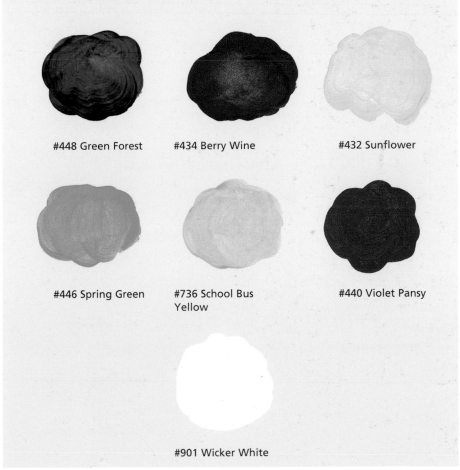

#448 Green Forest   #434 Berry Wine   #432 Sunflower

#446 Spring Green   #736 School Bus Yellow   #440 Violet Pansy

#901 Wicker White

This pattern may be hand-traced or photocopied for personal use only. Enlarge at 118% to return the image to full size.

~ *Constructing the Birdhouse Post* ~

1. Screw or nail the 12″-square (30cm-square) board to the bottom of the post. Be sure to center and secure the base.

2. Attach the birdhouse to the top of the post in a similar fashion. I pre-drilled screw holes in the post before attaching the birdhouse to it. You might want to attach a piece of 1″ stock to the post first, and then attach the birdhouse to the piece of stock.

3. Lightly sand the entire piece and wipe it clean.

4. Apply two coats of Wicker White using a sponge brush, and allow each coat to dry thoroughly.

5. Trace or transfer the pattern.

Pattern for post

This pattern may be hand-traced or photocopied for personal use only. Enlarge at 114% to return the image to full size.

Paint the Wild Rosebud

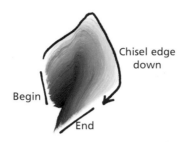

Wild Rosebud

Double load a no. 12 flat brush with Berry Wine and Wicker White.

Starting on the chisel edge, go to the point of the bud and slide down to the chisel edge as you come to the base of the bud.

Second Stroke of Wild Rosebud

Double load a no. 12 flat brush with Berry Wine and Wicker White.

Use the technique you just learned to paint another petal over the first petal.

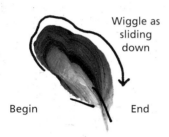

Opening Wild Rosebud (Petal)

Double load a no. 12 flat brush with Berry Wine and Wicker White.

Starting on the chisel edge, slide up and then slide down. As you are sliding down, wiggle the bristles and end on the chisel edge.

Opening Wild Rosebud (Layered Petals)

Repeating the steps for the first petal, paint more petals, one on top of the other.

Completed Opening Wild Rosebud

The bud is formed by overlaying the individual petals. Remember to paint with the darker color to the outside edge.

~ Vines and Stems ~

Double load a no. 12 flat brush with Spring Green and Green Forest.

Paint the vines and stems by pulling the chisel edge of the brush around the pole, leading with the Spring Green edge.

Paint the Wild Rose

Full Wild Rose (First Petal)

Double load a no. 12 flat brush with Berry Wine and Wicker White.

Starting on the chisel edge and pivoting from the base of the petal, push and wiggle the bristles to make "M"s on the outside edge of the petal. Keep the Berry Wine edge to the inside.

Full Wild Rose (Layered Petals)

Repeat brush-loading step.

Paint petals, one over another, to form an apron of petals.

Full Wild Rose (Variation)

The wild rose with the reverse color on the outside edge.

Completed Apron of Overlaid Petals

I overlaid six petals on this rose, but the number could be more. However, less than five may not make the rose look full enough.

Second Layer of Petals

Repeat the instructions for the outer apron of petals.

Paint this second layer of petals a little closer together.

Third Layer of Petals

Continue to paint the overlaying petals even closer together.

Center of Wild Rose

Load the scruffy brush with Green Forest and a touch of School Bus Yellow. Pounce up and down to form the center of the flower.

Completed Wild Rose

Notice the darker color towards the center. It makes the rose look tightly layered and full.

Paint Wild Rose Leaves

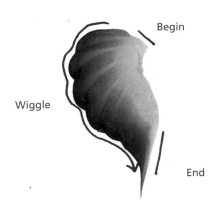

Wild Rose Leaf

Double load a no. 12 flat brush with Green Forest and Sunflower.

Starting on the chisel edge, push the bristles down, wiggling slightly, and then turn and lift the brush to its chisel edge.

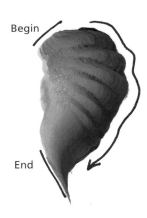

Second Half of Wild Rose Leaf

Repeat the steps you just learned.

Completed Leaf (Combined Halves)

An important point to remember is to form the ''V'' area at the top of the leaf. When you paint the two halves together, this space will allow the stem to lead more naturally from the leaf.

Finished Leaf With Stem

Double load a no. 12 flat brush with Green Forest and Sunflower.

Using the chisel edge, pull into the leaf at the ''V'' area to create the stem and to finish the leaf.

Tendrils (Curlicues)

Refer to chapter one, page 58.

Paint the Smaller Leaves

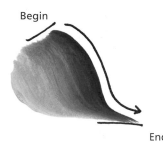

Begin

End

Smaller Leaves (One-Stroke Leaves)

Double load a no. 12 flat brush with Green Forest and Sunflower.

Remember, these are the leaves that are painted by pushing, turning and lifting the brush to its chisel edge. It's important to turn the green edge to form the tip of the leaf.

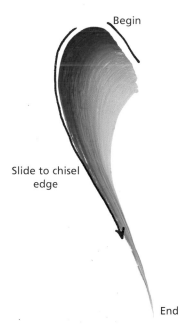

Begin

Slide to chisel edge

End

Alternative Wild Rose Leaf

Double load a no. 12 flat brush with Green Forest and Sunflower.

This leaf differs in that one side has a smooth edge instead of the wiggled edge. Paint the first half of the leaf as a "wiggled" leaf. Paint the second half by beginning on the chisel edge, pushing slightly and sliding the bristles back to the chisel edge. Lead with the lighter color.

Finished Alternative Leaf

Once again, remember to picture the "V" area at the top of this leaf. Starting on the chisel edge, slide a stem into the "V" center.

~ Donna's Hints ~

Remember to lead with the green on the outside edge. I remind you of this because as you paint the opposite side of the leaf, you will need to turn the brush. This may sound simple, but I can't recall how many times I've forgotten to do it!

Paint the Butterfly

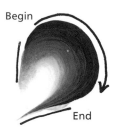

Begin

End

Butterfly Wing

Double load a no. 12 flat brush with Violet Pansy and Wicker White.

Starting on the chisel edge, slide the bristles upward to make a C-stroke, and slide back to the chisel edge. The violet should be on the out-side edge.

Layered Butterfly Wings

Repeat the step for the butterfly wings, layering the second wing on top of the first. This creates a double wing.

Bottom Wings of Butterfly

Double load a no. 12 flat brush with Violet Pansy and Wicker White.

Using the chisel edge, paint the bottom wings under the two top wings. Lead with the white edge.

Connecting Wings

The two bottom wings connected to two top, layered wings.

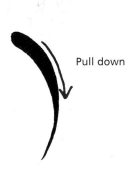

Pull down

Butterfly Body

Load a no. 2 script liner with Violet Pansy. Do not use water.

Using the tip of the bristles, pull down to form the body. To form the point at the base of the body, lift up as you complete the stroke.

Antennae

Load a no. 2 script liner with Violet Pansy. Do not use water.

If you divide this stroke into three parts, it will be much simpler to paint. First, using the tip of the bristles, paint the inner curl by bring-ing the brush around in a half-circle. Second, turn the brush to paint the outer turn of the cir-cle. Third, using the tip of the bristles and a light touch, paint the long part of the antennae.

Finished Butterfly

This is a simple butterfly, but I hope you can see the versatility of it. This butterfly can be painted quickly, so paint as many as you would like anywhere on the birdhouse.

Fruit Cabinet and Plates

I recently attended my son's wedding in the western part of the United States. While there, I found a wonderful variety of fruit. No matter what part of the country I am in, there is always special fruit that is indigenous to the area. I know I take pride in the citrus fruit from Florida. I am sure you take pride in the different varieties of fruit from your home state. I am pretty sure I have, at one time or another, painted every kind of fruit.

My inspiration for this cabinet was my need to decorate a room. I didn't want anything too formal. Fruit seemed to be the appropriate motif, so I designed a wall cabinet to store jars of jams and jellies. The plates make great accent pieces that tie in with thc theme. I chose to include apples, plums, pears and grapes in the design for their colors. They really brighten up the room. I added the lighter background leaves to soften the stark white of the cabinet. You can also paint a border to complete the theme.

Whenever I sit in my room, it seems to cheer me up. I hope you have as much fun painting this project as I did. Maybe next time you go to the supermarket or produce stand, you'll think of me.

~ Choosing Plates ~

Look for plates that are approximately 12" (30cm) in diameter. I chose plates without excessive scrollwork or edge routering that would interfere with my painting.

~ Materials ~

Wood cabinet: You'll need a cabinet approximately 21" wide × 8" deep × 24" high (53cm × 20cm × 61cm). I had a local woodworking shop build this cabinet. The arched door adds a touch of elegance to the cabinet, but I think it would work just as well with a straight-edged door. Remember to attach some kind of hanger on the reverse side of the cabinet so it can be hung on the wall.

Brushes: You'll need a ¾-inch (1.9cm) flat brush, a no. 12 flat brush and a no. 2 script liner. Once again, I used the FolkArt One-Stroke Brushes.

Sponge: Use a flat, all-purpose household sponge.

Transfer materials: You'll need some transfer/tracing paper and a stylus.

Sponge brush: Use a 1½" (3.8cm) sponge brush.

Sealer: I used #789 FolkArt Acrylic Sealer matte finish.

Good quality acrylic paints: I used FolkArt Acrylic Colors by Plaid. Colors needed for this project are shown below.

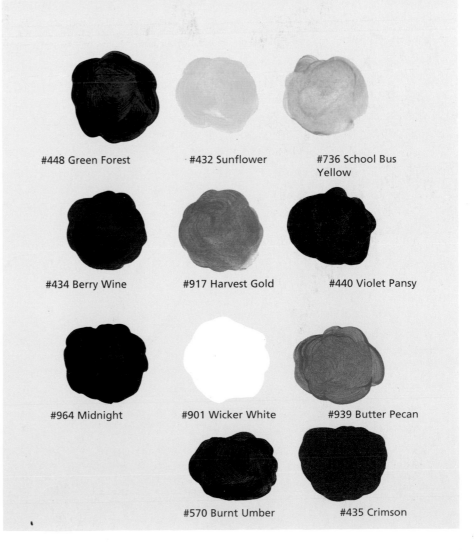

#448 Green Forest   #432 Sunflower   #736 School Bus Yellow

#434 Berry Wine   #917 Harvest Gold   #440 Violet Pansy

#964 Midnight   #901 Wicker White   #939 Butter Pecan

#570 Burnt Umber   #435 Crimson

Enlarge at 257% to
return the image to
full size

～ *Plate Preparation* ～

Use a sponge loaded with Wicker White and Butter Pecan to lightly pounce on the plate. Be sure to make a direct up-and-down motion, or the color will have a tendency to smear. Pounce the color as darkly or as lightly as you like.
Be creative!

Enlarge at 164% to
return the image to
full size.

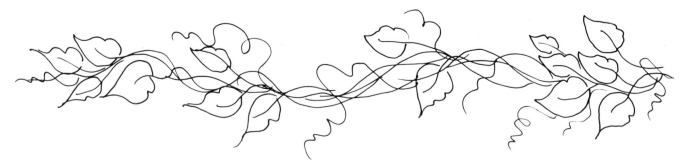

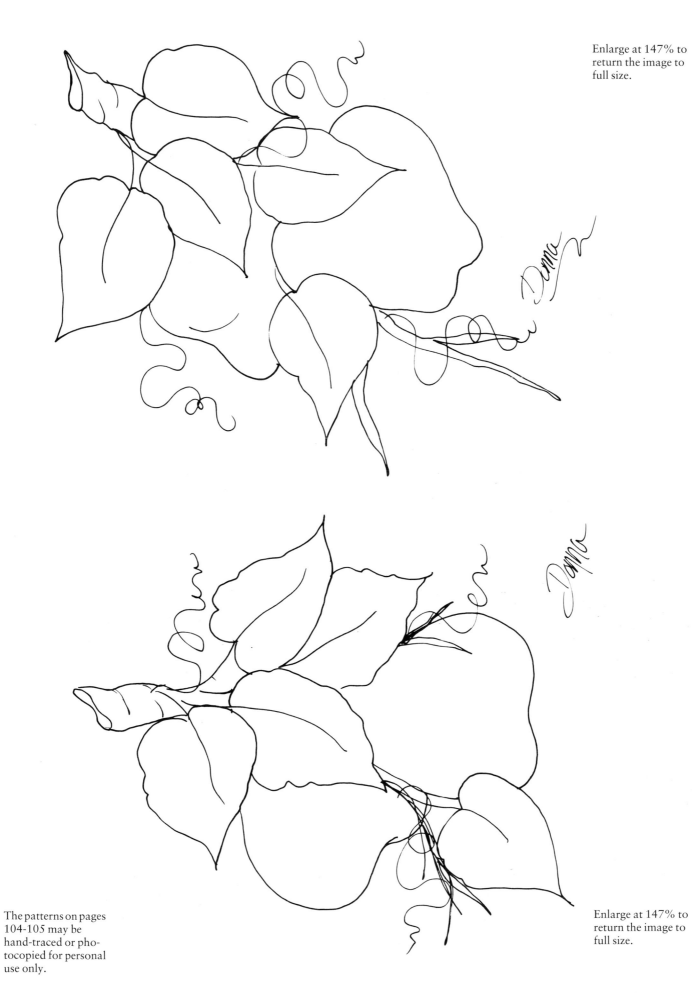

Enlarge at 147% to return the image to full size.

Enlarge at 147% to return the image to full size.

Fruit Cabinet and Plates 105

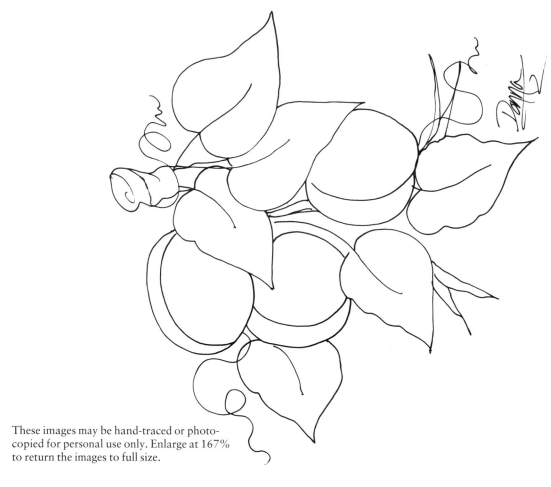

These images may be hand-traced or photo-copied for personal use only. Enlarge at 167% to return the images to full size.

Paint the Pear

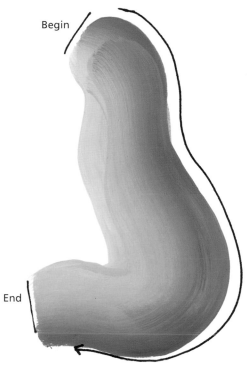

First Half of Pear

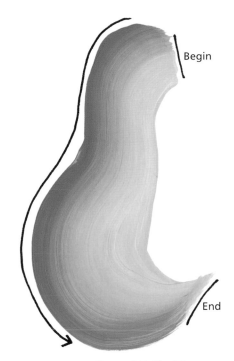

Second Half of Pear

Double load a ¾-inch (1.9cm) flat brush with School Bus Yellow and Harvest Gold, with just a touch of Berry Wine on the Harvest Gold edge. (Refer to the multi-loading technique in the beginning of this book.)

The pear is painted similar to the apple, only this time you need to paint a pear shape.

Repeat the steps you just learned. At this point, you need to form the base of the pear.

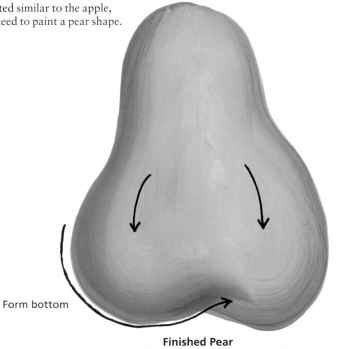

Finished Pear

While the paint is still wet, stroke from the center to create a smooth and three-dimensional pear.

Paint the Plum

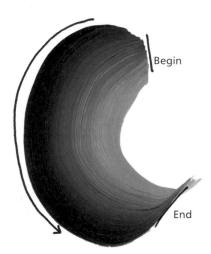

First Stroke of Plum

Multi-load a ¾-inch (1.9cm) flat brush with Midnight and Wicker White, with a touch of Berry Wine on the white edge.

Starting on the chisel edge with Midnight to the outside edge, make a large C-stroke to form the shape of the plum.

Second Stroke of Plum

Load the brush as directed for the first stroke of the plum.

Paint the same stroke about halfway over your first stroke.

Make sure the second stroke can be clearly seen.

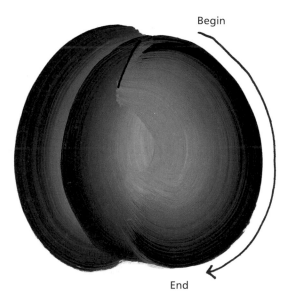

Third Stroke of Plum

Load the brush as directed for the first stroke of the plum.

Paint the third stroke all the way around the plum, forming the defining shape on one side. If the strokes are done properly, you will see the dividing line that shades the two halves.

Completed Plum

Gently stroke the brush back and forth while the paint is still wet to smooth the plum's surface.

Paint the Fruit Leaves and Stems

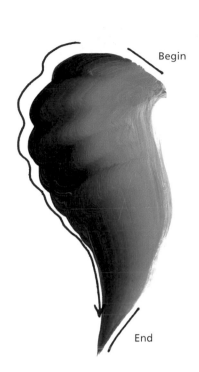

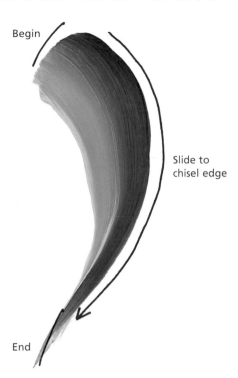

First Half of Fruit Leaf

Double load a ¾-inch (1.9cm) flat brush with Sunflower and Green Forest.

Starting on the chisel edge, push, wiggle slightly, and slide back to the chisel edge with the green to the outside edge of the leaf. I like to paint these leaves on top of the apples, pears and plums.

Second Half of Fruit Leaf

Double load a ¾-inch (1.9cm) flat brush with Sunflower and Green Forest.

Starting on the chisel edge, slide the edge with Sunflower along the inner edge of the leaf, all the way to the tip of the leaf.

Finished Leaf

The two halves form the fruit leaf. Notice that the shading and blending of the colors is similar to that of an actual fruit leaf. Remember to keep the brush loaded properly, or this effect will be difficult to obtain.

Smooth-Textured Fruit Leaf

Double load a ¾-inch (1.9cm) flat brush with Sunflower and Green Forest.

Begin painting on the chisel edge. To form the leaf, push down on the brush to spread the bristles. As you complete the stroke, lift the brush to its chisel edge. This will form the point of the leaf. Keep the green to the outside edge.

Second Half of Smooth-Textured Fruit Leaf

Repeat the steps you just learned for the second half. Keep the green to the outside edge.

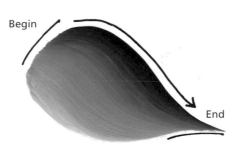

Finished Smooth-Textured Fruit Leaf

Be sure to maintain a sharp point on the leaf tip when you combine the two strokes.

One-Stroke Leaf

Refer to chapter three, page 76, for instructions on painting One-Stroke leaves.

Stems for One-Stroke Leaves

Load a no. 12 flat brush with Sunflower and Green Forest. Pull into the leaf on the chisel edge, leading with the lighter color.

Small Cluster of Filler Leaves

Double load a no. 12 flat brush with Sunflower and Green Forest.
    Starting on the chisel edge, in one sweeping stroke create a leaf. Keep the green to the outside edge.

Fruit Stems

Double load a no. 12 flat brush with Sunflower and Green Forest.
    Use the chisel edge to paint the fruit stems. Start underneath the fruit and stroke into the leaves, leading with the Sunflower edge.

Paint the Grapes

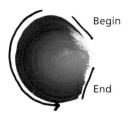 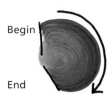

Begin

End

Begin

End

Starting the Grapes

Load a no. 12 flat brush with Violet Pansy and a touch of Midnight. I pick up a small amount of Berry Wine every so often to add just a hint of another color to the grapes.

It isn't necessary to paint complete grapes, because they will be layered. Paint the first half of the grapes, and then layer one over another. If you want to see a whole grape, then you will need to make a complete circle (refer to directions for whole grape).

Starting on the chisel edge, make a C-stroke with the darker color to the outside edge.

Whole Grape

Combine the strokes of two grape halves to complete a whole grape. You may have to flip the brush over and gently stroke back and forth to smooth the grape.

Different Colors of Grapes

You may want to add lighter colors to the inner grapes and darker colors to the outer grapes. This is up to you. As you can see, it sometimes helps to define the grapes.

Finished grapes in different colors.

Layer grapes over one another.

Finish the Project

Create Shadow

To create the shadow on the plates, float a small amount of Maple Syrup on the edge of the leaves and on one side of the fruit. Side load a ¾-inch (1.9cm) flat brush with Maple Syrup, and lightly stroke it as directed in the One-Stroke Techniques section, page 48.

Tendrils (Curlicues)

Refer to chapter one, page 58.

This is how your finished Fruit Cabinet should look.

Notice how the watercolor leaves are placed on the top and sides of the cabinet.

The completed apple plate.

The completed pear plate.

The completed plum plate.

The completed grape plate.

Bouquet of Roses Serving Tray

I think Roses are the most elegant of all flowers. They come in so many varieties, and the colors seem innumerable. Roses are named for famous people (*Queen Elizabeth*), for yummy foods (*Pink Parfait*), and for wonderful values and ideas (*Peace Rose*). My painting career was inspired, in part, by my desire to paint roses. I can remember thinking that if I could master the art of painting roses, I would feel as though I had reached an incredible level. To me, roses seem to embody special standards of beauty and quality. We all try to attain this kind of beauty and quality at some time or another.

∾ Materials ∾

Wooden tray: You'll need a tray approximately 18″ long × 12″ wide × 3″ high (46cm × 30cm × 8cm). I purchased this tray from a local woodworking shop. The materials to make the tray are readily available in lumber supply stores.

Brushes: You'll need a ¾-inch (1.9cm) flat brush, a no. 12 flat brush and a no. 2 script liner.

Sponge: You'll need a flat all-purpose household sponge.

Transfer materials: You'll need some transfer/tracing paper and a stylus.

Sponge brush: Use a 1½-inch (3.8cm) sponge brush.

Sealer: I used #789 FolkArt Acrylic Sealer —matte finish.

Good quality acrylic paints: I used FolkArt Acrylic Colors by Plaid. Colors needed for this project are shown below.

#434 Berry Wine

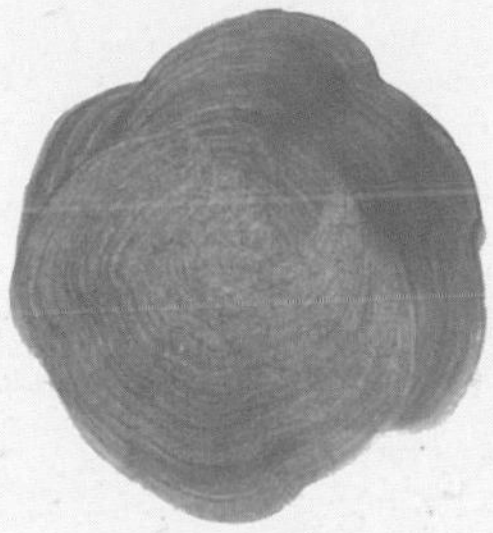

#917 Harvest Gold

#747 Salmon

#440 Violet Pansy

#432 Sunflower

#448 Green Forest

#939 Butter Pecan

#901 Wicker White

∾ Donna's Hints ∾

Remember, you can paint wet paint on top of wet paint, because you are not using water (which would muddy the strokes).

Paint the Filler Flowers

Begin — End

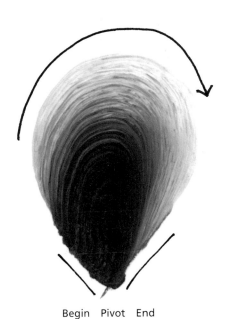

Begin   Pivot   End

C-Stroke Filler Flowers

**Combining C-Stroke
Petals to Form a Flower**

Double load a no. 12 flat brush with Wicker White and Violet Pansy.

Stroke from the tip of the cluster downward, layering as you paint. Paint with the chisel edge in short strokes, lifting the brush to its chisel edge. Picturing a small teardrop will help you visualize the shape of this stroke.

Double load a no. 12 flat brush with Wicker White and Violet Pansy.

Begin and end on the chisel edge, pivoting the stroke from the base to form a "C" shape.

Follow the previous instructions, and layer these petals to form the flower. You will find that combining four or more of these petals will make a good flower.

Finished C-Stroke Flower

Make the center of the flower by dipping the handle end of the no. 12 flat brush into School Bus Yellow. Dot the center, where the petals meet.

Finish

Watercolor-Effect Leaves, Stems and Vines in Background and Edge of Tray

Side load the no. 12 flat brush with water and Butter Pecan. Paint the stems and vines by pulling on the chisel edge into the leaves.

This is one of those rare instances where I mix water with the paint. You will need to side load a no. 12 flat brush with Butter Pecan and a small amount of water. Blend the paint into the brush until the bristles are at least two-thirds full. Paint little One-Stroke leaves as described on page 35.

Tendrils (Curlicues)

Refer to chapter one, page 58.

This is how your completed tray should look.
Notice the placement of the roses.

Resources

Plaid Enterprises

1649 International Ct.

Box 600

Norcross, GA 30091

Cabin Crafters

1225 W. First St.

Nevada, IA 50201

Dewberry Designs

811 E. Highland Dr.

Alamonte Springs, FL 32701

For information on any One-Stroke products:

Fax: (407) 831-0658

E-mail: dewberry@magicnet.net

Website: www.onestroke.com

Index

Antiquing, 49-51

Basecoating, 12
Berries, 90
Birdhouse, 25-27, 56-60, 93-102
Bouquet of Roses Serving Tray, 117-125
Bow, 45-46, 73, 82
Branch, 42, 87, 107
Brush, 10
  cleaning and caring for, 10
  handle for making dots, 23
  holding, 16-17
  loading, 18-24
  "M" motion, 37
  parts of, 16
  side loading, 23
  See also specific types of brushes
Buds
  magnolia, 89
  See also Rosebuds
Butterfly, 100

Clay pots, 63-70
C-stroke, 34, 123
Curlicues, 43, 76, 83, 107

Daisy, 28-29, 65-66

Flat brush, 16, 18-20
Floorcloth, 13, 85-92
Flower
  centers, 24-28
  C-stroke, 34
  filler, 123
  leaves, 35-41
  petals, 29, 60
  stalk, 60
  See also specific types of flowers
Fruit Cabinet and Plates, 103-116

Garden Birdhouse Mailbox, 53-63. See
    also Birdhouse

Grapevines, 42, 81. See also Vines
Grass, 43, 58-60

Ivy, 39, 74-76
Ivy Keepsake Box, 13, 49-51, 71-78

Lacquer finish, 61
Leaf
  all-in-one, 38
  basic, 35
  fruit, 107, 111-112
  ivy, 39, 75-76
  magnolia, 90
  one-stroke, 38, 58, 67
  rose, 83, 98-99, 122
  scallop-edged, 36
  "slide," 39
  sunflower, 40
  turned-edge, 41
Lettering, 81

Magnolia Floorcloth and Door Crown,
    85-92
Mailbox, 12, 53-63
Moss, 57, 59, 65

One-Stroke Techniques, 14-15, 16-51

Paint, 10
Palette, 18
Petal
  chisel-edge, 29
  C-stroke, 34
  daisy, 29
  narrow, 60
  rose, 30, 97, 119
  sunflower, 24
Plates, 103-116
Pouncing, 44

Ribbon, 45-46, 82
Rose, 117-120, 122

cabbage, 33
  wild, 28, 97. See also Wild Rose
    Birdhouse
Rosebud, 30-32, 82, 96, 119-121
Rosebud Memory Album, 79-84

Script liner, 17, 22
Scruffy brush, 17, 21
Serving tray, 117-125
Shading, 48
Shadowing, 48, 114
Shell stroke, 33
Sponging, 44
Stem
  fruit, 112
  ivy, 76
  leaf, 38, 67
  rose, 32, 96-97, 121
Sunflower, 24-27, 40
Supplies, 10-11
Surface, preparing, 12

Techniques. See One-Stroke Techniques
Tendrils, 58. See also Curlicues
Terra-cotta pot, 12

Vines, 58, 67, 43
  fruit, 107
  ivy, 74
  rose, 96
  See also Grapevines

Watering can, 63-70
Wildflower, center, 28
Wild Rose Birdhouse, 93-102
Wisteria, 44, 57, 68
Wood, preparing, 13

More Great Books for Decorative Painters!

Acrylic Decorative Painting Techniques—Discover stroke-by-stroke instruction that takes you through the basics and beyond! More than 50 fun and easy painting techniques are illustrated in simple demonstrations that offer at least two variations on each method. Plus, a thorough discussion on tools, materials, color, preparation and backgrounds. #30884/$24.99/128 pages/550 color illus.

Painting & Decorating Birdhouses—Turn unfinished birdhouses into something special—from a quaint Victorian roost to a Southwest pueblo, from a rustic log cabin to a lighthouse! These colorful and easy decorative painting projects are for the birds with 22 clever projects to create indoor decorative birdhouses, as well as functional ones to grace your garden. #30882/$23.99/128 pages/194 color illus./paperback

Decorative Painting Sourcebook—Priscilla Hauser, Phillip Myer and Jackie Shaw lend their expertise to this one-of-a-kind guide straight from the pages of Decorative Artist's Workbook! You'll find step-by-step, illustrated instructions on every technique—from basic brushstrokes to faux finishes, painting glassware, wood, clothing and much more! #30883/$24.99/128 pages/200 color illus./paperback

The Decorative Stamping Sourcebook—Embellish walls, furniture, fabric and accessories—with stamped designs! You'll find 180 original, traceable motifs in a range of themes and illustrated instructions for making your own stamps to enhance any decorating style. #30898/$24.99/128 pages/200 color illus.

Master Strokes—Master the techniques of decorative painting with this comprehensive guide! Learn to use decorative paint finishes on everything from small objects and furniture to walls and floors, including dozens of step-by-step demonstrations and numerous techniques. #30937/$22.99/160 pages/400 color illus./paperback

The Best of Silk Painting—Discover inspiration in sophisticated silk with this gallery of free-flowing creativity. Over 100 full-color photos capture the glorious colors, unusual textures and unique designs of 77 talented artists. #30840/$29.99/128 pages/136 color illus.

Decorative Painting With Gretchen Cagle—Discover decorative painting at its finest as you browse through pages of charming motifs. You'll brighten walls, give life to old furniture, create unique accent pieces and special gifts using step-by-step instructions, traceable drawings, detailed color mixes and more! #30803/$24.99/144 pages/64 color, 36 b&w illus./paperback

Painting Houses, Cottages and Towns on Rocks—Discover how a dash of paint can turn humble stones into charming cottages, churches, Victorian mansions and more. This hands-on, easy-to-follow book offers a menagerie of fun—and potentially profitable—stone animal projects. Eleven examples, complete with material list, photos of the finished piece and patterns will help you create entire rock villages. #30823/$21.99/128 pages/398 color illus./paperback

Creative Paint Finishes for Furniture—Revive your furniture with fresh color and design! Inexpensive, easy and fun painting techniques are at your fingertips, along with step-by-step directions and a photo gallery of imaginative applications for faux finishing, staining, stenciling, mosaic, découpage and many other techniques. #30748/$27.99/144 pages/236 color, 7 b&w illus.

Creative Paint Finishes for the Home—A complete, full-color step-by-step guide to decorating floors, walls and furniture—including how to use the tools, master the techniques and develop ideas. #30426/$27.99/144 pages/212 color illus.

Master Works: How to Use Paint Finishes to Transform Your Surroundings—Discover how to use creative paint finishes to enhance and excite the "total look" of your home. This step-by-step guide contains dozens of exciting ideas on fresco, marbling, paneling and other simple paint techniques for bringing new life to any space. Plus, you'll also find innovative uses for fabrics, screens and blinds. #30626/$29.95/176 pages/150 color illus.

Paint Craft—Discover great ideas for enhancing your home, wardrobe and personal items. You'll see how to master the basics of mixing and planning colors, how to print with screen and linoleum to create your own stationery, how to enhance old glassware and pottery pieces with unique patterns and motifs and much more! #30678/$16.95/144 pages/200 color illus./paperback

Create Your Own Greeting Cards and Gift Wrap with Priscilla Hauser—You'll see sponge prints, eraser prints, cellophane scrunching, marbleizing, paper making and dozens of other techniques you can use to make unique greetings for all your loved ones. #30621/$24.99/128 pages/230 color illus.

Stencil Source Book 2—Add color and excitement to fabrics, furniture, walls and more with over 200 original motifs that can be used again and again! Idea-packed chapters will help you create dramatic color schemes and themes to enhance your home in hundreds of ways. #30730/$22.99/144 pages/300 illus.

The Crafts Supply Sourcebook, 4th edition—Turn here to find the materials you need—from specialty tools and the hardest-to-find accessories, to clays, doll parts, patterns, quilting machines and hundreds of other items! Listings organized by area of interest make it quick and easy! #70344/$18.99/320 pages/paperback

Nature Craft—Dozens of step-by-step nature craft projects to create, including dried flower garlands, baskets, corn dollies, potpourri and more. Bring the outdoors inside with these wonderful projects crafted with readily available natural materials. #30531/$16.99/144 pages/200 color illus./paperback

Paper Craft—Dozens of step-by-step paper craft projects to make, including greeting cards, boxes and desk sets, jewelry and pleated paper blinds. If you have ever worked with or wanted to work with paper you'll enjoy these attractive, fun-to-make projects. #30530/$16.95/144 pages/200 color illus./paperback

Painting Murals—Learn through eight step-by-step projects how to choose a subject for a mural, select colors that will create the desired effects and transfer the design to the final surface. #30081/$29.99/168 pages/125 color illus.